PKD
A
Philip K. Dick
Bibliography

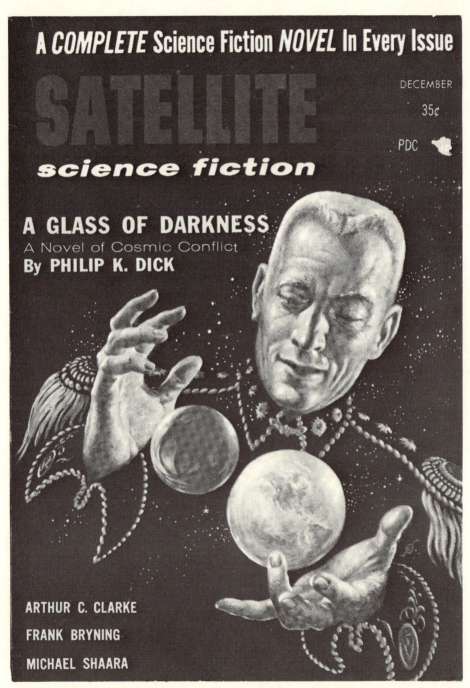

A **COMPLETE** Science Fiction **NOVEL** In Every Issue

SATELLITE
science fiction

DECEMBER

35¢

PDC

A GLASS OF DARKNESS
A Novel of Cosmic Conflict
By **PHILIP K. DICK**

ARTHUR C. CLARKE

FRANK BRYNING

MICHAEL SHAARA

"A Glass Of Darkness" — *first magazine appearance. (See page 96, item 42.a.)*

PKD

A
PHILIP K. DICK
BIBLIOGRAPHY

Compilied by
Daniel J H Levack

with
Annotations
by
Steven Owen Godersky

UNDERWOOD/MILLER
San Francisco, California
Columbia, Pennsylvania
1981

PKD: A Philip K. Dick Bibliography

PHOTOGRAPHY FOR THIS BIBLIOGRAPHY BY PAUL A. NELSON

To
Sandra

TABLE OF CONTENTS

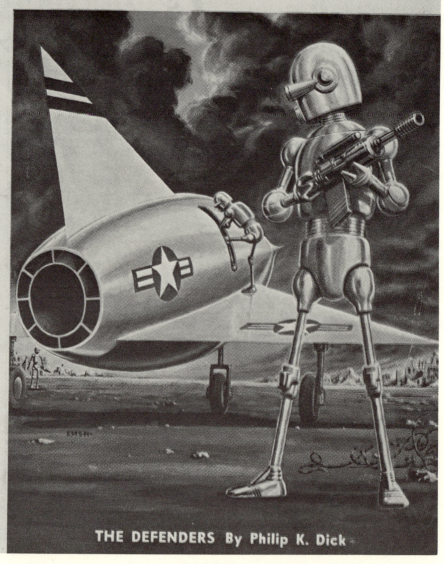

Galaxy
SCIENCE FICTION

JANUARY 1953
35¢

ANC

THE DEFENDERS By Philip K. Dick

"The Defenders" — first magazine appearance. (See page 89, item 25.a.)

INTRODUCTION

This bibliography attempts to cite all the published works of Philip K Dick through mid 1981. Both foreign and English language publications are included. Fictional and non-fictional works and published interviews are also covered, but there is no intent to be inclusive in listing Dick's published letters.

This attempt at completeness is not entirely successful. Dick has been published extensively in both foreign languages and foreign countries and it has proven difficult to achieve completeness in this area. Although the bibliography does cite translations into 19 foreign languages and publication in 26 foreign countries, some languages and countries have probably been totally missed and the coverage is much more thorough for some languages than for others. Specifically, foreign language book editions are cited very extensively but foreign language story appearances, because of their more elusive nature (here in the United States at least), have certainly not all been found. Nevertheless, 214 foreign language book editions and 205 foreign language story appearances are taken into account. The bibliography probably is complete in English language first appearances and it is missing few English language book editions and story appearances through 1980. The net result is a Philip K Dick bibliography considerably more extensive than any previously published and much of the credit for this is attributable to Phil Dick's active help, which led to the location of many items that otherwise would have been omitted.

A number of features supplement the factual text, in an attempt to make this bibliography more useful and entertaining. Descriptive annotations by Steve Godersky are included, as are selected annotations by Philip K Dick (all of Dick's are in quotes and are taken with his permission from previously published sources). Physical descriptions are given for the majority of hardcover books and likewise for paperbacks where there is something unusual about the edition. For the benefit of collectors, the covers of approximately 190 citations are reproduced as photographs. Series and connected stories and related milieus are denoted, as is Dick's single pseudonymous appearance.

Also, a great deal of unpublished material is listed, along with Dick's appearances in other media (this latter is considerably lacking in detail). A non-fiction index and a verse index are included, the works are cross-indexed in chronological order and a magazine issue checklist is included for the collector.

An incomplete, though still extensive, secondary bibliography is included to round out the presentation.

The majority of the approximately 1000 citations have been physically examined by myself. An additional small number were examined by Steve Godersky or Jeff Levin but not by myself. All physically examined citations (over 725) are marked with an "*" at the end of the citation.

For a new printing of a book to be included as a new citation it was required that something about the edition, other than a simple statement of the printing, be changed; e.g., the cover, book number, price, title or some such must have been altered. When the only change was a statement such as "Second printing" or the removal of a first edition statement then it is noted by the phrase "Reprinted 1977, 1979" or as appropriate under the affected citation. No doubt a number of simple reprintings have been omitted.

For a citation to be included in the STORIES section it had to represent a new choice to publish the cited work. Consequently, only the first printing of anthologies or collections is given; paperback editions of hardcover editions and reprints are not separately cited or normally even mentioned. There are two exceptions to this inclusion rule. First, if the reprints do not include the cited work, that will be mentioned. (It is not uncommon for paperback reprints of hardcover anthologies to drop some stories.) Second, foreign language translations of anthologies and collections are included since there is nothing automatic about foreign language editions and they thus represent a new choice to publish the cited work (often the first or only appearance in a given language). However, reprints of these anthologies and collections are not separately cited in the STORIES section.

In the physical description of states of an edition, if a state has been seen it is simply described, but if the information is from some other source it is introduced as "According to L W Currey . . ." or "Tim Underwood has seen . . ." or as appropriate to avoid the impression of an independent confirmation of other data. Within these descriptions anything in quotes will actually be found printed in the item cited, with the convention that a double slash, //, within a quote means that the text drops to a new line (a single slash, /, simply means there is a slash in the text quoted—see VALIS).

Within the body of the bibliography an all-upper-case title represents a book, a title with both upper and lower case characters a periodical, and a title enclosed in quotes a story (i.e., anything, including a novel, which appeared in a periodical, an anthology or a collection). For all entries (excepting periodicals) the lack of the word "paper" implies a hard-bound edition. The bibliographic format for entries is:

a. *for hardbound books*
   TITLE, EDITOR (if appropriate), PUBLISHER, PLACE OF PUBLICATION (PRICE), YEAR OF PUBLICATION.
b. *for paperbound books*
   TITLE, EDITOR (if appropriate), PUBLISHER: BOOK NUMBER (PRICE), YEAR OF PUBLICATION, "paper".
c. *for periodicals*
   TITLE, DATE (sometimes also or instead a Volume and Number and/or a whole issue number).

Where manuscript titles are given they are either from the manuscript collection at the California State University, Fullerton, or from the author. Where a word count is given it is from the manuscript collection, Tim Underwood's count, a specific statement by a magazine of the count, or Norm Metcalf's THE INDEX OF SCIENCE FICTION MAGAZINES 1951-1965.

Additions and corrections to the bibliography are both desired and welcome, as are comments on format and content. All such can be sent to:

> *Daniel J H Levack*
> *7745 Jason Ave*
> *Canoga Park, California 91304*
> *USA*

—Daniel J H Levack
1981

ANNOTATOR'S NOTE:
   When I was asked to annotate the bibliography of Philip K Dick I was elated at having the opportunity to contribute to such a personally meaningful undertaking. Only later did I begin to appreciate the magnitude and complexity of the task I had so cheerfully assumed. My personal collection of Phil Dick's works was extensive but not totally complete, and here Dan and Tim offered generous and invaluable assistance. I turned to reexamine the books and digests I possessed with an optimistic heart.
   During the earliest part of my readings, however, it began to dawn on me that perhaps I had blindly succumbed to hubris, the pride that destroyeth. Here I was, attempting to characterize in a few short

phrases the writings of an author incomparably more talented than myself. How could I ensure that I had even grasped the essentials of Phil Dick's ideas, much less his complex style and nuances of meanings? How could I dispose of a vastly talented writer's life works in the limits that had been set? The answer was, of course, that I could not.

The ultimate intention behind the annotation of this bibliography is not to tell what the stories **mean***, but simply to give an indication of what they are* **about***. My remarks may serve, hopefully, as a reminder of the settings of the stories; they may act as a very short indication of development and plot, (though here, I am afraid, they are very incomplete) and they may briefly allow the interested reader to recall in his own mind tales he has already enjoyed, with a view to comparison or reexamination. I hope that the graphic crudity and glaring omissions within the annotations will be excused in the same spirit in which one refrains from criticizing a charcoal sketch of the Sistine Chapel ceiling, which the artist has at best intended as a reminder of the artistry or a rough placement of figures to allow later contemplation of the truly serene beauties of the original.*

—Steven Owen Godersky
1981

Abbreviations:

Ed - Edited
No - Number
sr# - serial in # parts
Vol - Volume

PKD

A
Philip K. Dick
Bibliography

WORLD OF CHANCE — *first edition. (See page 59, item 38.b.)*

BOOKS

1. THE BEST OF PHILIP K. DICK

Edited by John Brunner.

Contents: The Reality Of Philip K. Dick (by John Brunner); Beyond Lies the Wub; Roog; Second Variety; Paycheck; Impostor; Colony; Expendable; The Days Of Perky Pat; Breakfast At Twilight; Forster, You're Dead; The Father-Thing; Service Call; Autofac; Human Is; If There Were No Benny Cemoli; Oh, To Be A Blobel!; Faith Of Our Fathers; The Electric Ant; A Little Something For Us Tempunauts; Afterthoughts By The Author.

a. _____, Ballantine: 25359 ($1.95), 1977, paper.*
Reprinted 1978*

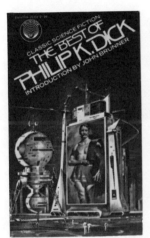 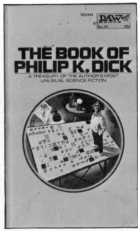 

1.a.   3.a.   3.b.

2. BISHOP TIMOTHY ARCHER

a. _____, Simon and Schuster.

Forthcoming. This is a fiction, but not a science fiction, novel. It is also the third, and final, book of the VALIS trilogy. It is scheduled for release in Spring 1982 as a Timescape hardcover book. The publisher has tentatively changed the title to THE TRANSMIGRATION OF BISHOP TIMOTHY ARCHER.

3. THE BOOK OF PHILIP K. DICK

Contents: Nanny; The Turning Wheel; The Defenders; Adjustment Team; Psi-Man; The Commuter; A Present For Pat; Breakfast At Twilight; Shell Game.

a. _____, DAW: 44 ($0.95), 1973, paper. Also numbered UQ1044.*
The US first printing is marked "FIRST PRINTING, FEBRUARY 1973" on the copyright page. However, it also is marked with a vertical string "FIRST PRINTING", "SECOND PRINTING" and so on through "TENTH PRINTING". The Canadian edition, which is marked "Printed in Canada" contains only the first printing statement.

b. (as THE TURNING WHEEL), Coronet: 21829 (80p), 1977.*

c. (I DIFENSORI DELLA TERRA) [Italian], Fanucci: Futuro 34, (L4000), 1977, paper.*
Translators: M Nati and S Pergameno.
Adds Oh, To Be A Blobel!; Retreat Syndrome; and We Can Remember It For You Wholesale.

4.a.   4.e.   4.j.

4. CLANS OF THE ALPHANE MOON

Chuck Rittersdorf is a CIA agent who has been duped by his hateful wife into moonlighting for a comedian in the pay of aliens. Betrayed on all sides, Chuck's only refuge is Alphane, a former hospital colony for psychotics. He is accompanied by his advisor, a telepathic slime-mold. All of Rittersdorf's enemies and allies meet on the psychotic planetoid, to settle their own differences and also to negotiate the Terran-Alphane war.

a. _____, Ace: F-309 ($0.40), 1964, paper.*

b. (FOLLIA PER SETTE CLAN) [Italian], Galassia: 124 (L350), 1970, paper.
Translators: V Curtoni and G Montanari.

c. _____, Ace: 11306 ($0.75), 1972, paper.*

d. (LES CLANS DE LA LUNE ALPHANE) [French], Albin Michel: 18, 1973, paper.*
Translator: François Truchaud.

e. _____, Panther: 04159 (50p), 1975, paper.*

f. (LES CLANS DE LA LUNE ALPHANE) [French], J'ai Lu: 879, 1978, paper.*
Translator: François Truchaud.

g. (DE ZEVEN CLANS VAN DE ALPHAANSE MAAN) [Dutch], Meulenhoff: SF 131, 1978, paper.*

h. (KLEINER MOND FÜR PSYCHOPATHEN) [German], Bastei-Lubbe: 22012 (DM 4.80), 1979, paper.*

i. _____, Gregg Press, Boston ($12.95), 1979.*
Introduction by Robert Silverberg. Frontispiece by Hannah Shapero. Bound in dark green cloth with gold lettering on the spine. Title and author's name are on bright red background on the spine. Author's signature stamped in gold on the front cover. "First printing, November 1979" on the copyright page. Issued without dustjacket. Text is photo-reproduced from the 1964 Ace edition.

j. _____, Dell: 11084 ($1.95), 1980, paper.*

4.h.

4.i. — *frontis and title page.*

5. CONFESSIONS OF A CRAP ARTIST

A mainstream fiction novel told from several viewpoints, including those of Jack Isidore, a borderline psychotic; Fay Isidore Hume; Charley Hume and Nathan Antheil. The story concerns life in West Marin County, California; including observations on modern life, infidelity and a UFO-watchers group.

a. _____, Entwhistle Books, New York ($10.00), 1975.*

b. _____, Entwhistle Books, ($5.95), 1977, paper.*
Introduction by Paul Williams.

The 1000 sets of sheets for "a" and "b" were printed together. 500 were bound in maroon cloth with gold lettering on the spine with the letters "P.K.D." stamped in gold on the front cover; 90 of these were numbered, and signed by Dick on the copyright page. These 500 hardbound copies were issued without a dustjacket. The remaining 500 sets of sheets were later bound and sold as trade paperbacks with an original cover by Richard Powers. 500 sets of sheets were printed with the statement "First edition" and 500 sets without. The 90 copy signed and numbered edition sold for $25.00.

c. _____, Entwhistle Books, ($3.95), 1978, paper.*
This second printing is identified on the copyright page and has a new cover. 5000 copies printed.

d. (CONFESSIONS D'UN BARJO) [French], Laffont (45.00F), 1978, paper.*
Translator: Janine Herisson.

e. _____, Magnum: 04290 (£1.25), 1979, paper.*

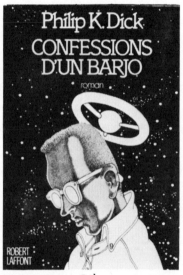

5.e.   5.d.   6.a.

6. THE COSMIC PUPPETS

("A Glass Of Darkness", Satellite, Dec 1956)
Ted Barton returns to the isolated town of his youth. He finds it subtly different. Places and people have been added and taken away. Some inhabitants have strange god-like powers. The intelligence controlling the town will not not let anyone escape.

a. _____, Ace: D-249 ($0.35), 1957, paper; with SARGASSO OF SPACE (Andrew North).*

b. (LA CITTA SOSTITUITA) [Italian], Urania: 280 (L150), 1962, paper.*
Translator: Luciana Piccolo Cattozzo.

c. _____, Berkley.
Purchased by Berkley but not yet scheduled.

7. COUNTER-CLOCK WORLD

Manuscript title "The Dead Grow Young".

The Hobart Phase has the effect of reversing entropy: bodies revive in the grave, the old grow younger, inventions are forgotten and books are unwritten. The institutions of power are the Vitariums, which sell the old people when they revive; a socio-religious movement called the FNM; and the Library, which is rumoured to illegally preserve knowledge doomed to be undiscovered. Representatives of all three institutions are waging an undeclared war over the body and soul of the newly revived Anarch Peak, the former and future leader of the FNM. (This novel was expanded from the story: "Your Appointment will be Yesterday.")

7.a. 7.f. 7.b.

a. _____, Berkley: X1372 ($0.60), 1967, paper.*

b. _____, Sphere: 29564 (5/-), 1968, paper.*

c. (A REBROUSSE-TEMPS) [French], Opta, Paris (31.00F), 1968.*
Translator: Michel Deutsh. Introduction by John Brunner. Illustrated. Combined with NOW WAIT FOR LAST YEAR. Bound in green cloth with gold lettering on the spine. Large logo stamped in gold on the front cover. Dick's copy has no dustjacket.

d. (REGRESSO AO PASSADO) [Portuguese], Panorama: EP-A-8 (20$), 1969(?), paper.*
Translator: J M Ferreirinha.

e. (GYAKUMAWARI NO SEKAI) [Japanese], Hayakawa Shobo (Y400), 1971, paper.
Translator: Obi Fusa.

f. (REDIVIVI S.p.A.) [Italian], Dall'Oglio: 4, Milan (L2000), 1972.*
Translator: Maria Silva. Pictorial cover.
Issued without dustjacket. Introduction by Inisero Cremaschi.

g. _____, Berkley: 02568 ($0.95), 1974, paper.*

h. (A REBROUSSE-TEMPS) [French], J'ai Lu: 613, 1975, paper.*
Translator: Michel Deutsh.

i. (DIE ZEIT LAUFT ZURÜCH) [German], Goldmann: 0248, 1977, paper.*

j. _____, Coronet: 21830 (70p), 1977, paper.

k. _____, Gregg Press, Boston ($11.95), 1979.*
Introduction by David G Hartwell. Frontispiece by Hannah Shapero.
Bound in dark green cloth with gold lettering on the spine. Title and
author's name are on bright red background on the spine. Author's
signature stamped in gold on front cover. "First Printing, April 1979"
on the copyright page. Issued without dustjacket. Text is photo-
reproduced from the 1967 Berkley edition.

8. **THE CRACK IN SPACE**

("Cantata 140", Fantasy & Science Fiction, July 1964, forms the first half of
this title.)

**Frozen sleep seems like a humane way to end unemployment and over-
population pressures: Send the excess citizens to the future. The government warehouses are filled with bibs when a political fight erupts
over whether or not to dispose of them through a space-warp. Then
some unknown outside agency helps the sleepers to awake.**

a. _____, Ace: F-377 ($0.40), 1966, paper.*

b. (VEDERE UN ALTRO ORIZZONTE) [Italian], Galassia: 99 (L350), 1969,
paper.*
Translator: Luigi Dancelli.

c. (BRÈCHE DANS L'ESPACE) [French], Gerard, 1974, paper (?).
Translator: Christian Meistermann. Published in Belgium.

d. _____, Ace: 12126 ($0.95), 1974, paper.*

e. (BRÈCHE DANS L'ESPACE) [French], Marabout: 477, 1975, paper.*
Translator: Christian Meistermann. Published in Belgium.

f. _____, Magnum: 36530 (70p), 1977, paper.*

g. (VEDERE UN ALTRO ORIZZONTE) [Italian], Tascabili Bompiani 150
(L2000), 1979, paper.*
Translator: Luigi Dancelli.

h. _____, Magnum: 05830 (£1.10), 1980, paper.

8.*a.*   8.*e.*   9.*a.*

9. LES DÉLIRES DIVERGENTS DE PHILIP K. DICK

Edited by Alain Doremieux.

French collection.

Contents: Roog; The Indefatigable Frog; The Crawlers; Captive Market; War Game; What The Dead Men Say; Precious Artifact; Retreat Syndrome; Return Match; The Pre-Persons.

a. _____, Casterman, Paris (?), 1979.*
Bound in tan paper boards with simulated cloth weave and with purple lettering on the front cover and on the spine.

10. DEUS IRAE

(with Roger Zelazny)

Manuscript title "The Kneeling Legless Man".

The atomic war which mostly destroyed the Earth is known to have been caused by the God of Wrath, one Carleton Lufteufel. His church is in the ascendant among the survivors. Tibor McMasters, legless and armless but still the best painter of the age, is sent by the Servants of Wrath to meet Carleton Lufteufel and paint his likeness. (Parts of this book were adapted from short stories titled: "The Great C" and "A Planet For Transients.")

a. _____, Doubleday, Garden City ($5.95), 1976.*
Bound in black paper boards with red lettering on the spine. Date code "G 27" (27th week of 1976) appears at the lower left margin of page 181. States "First Edition" on the copyright page. "1976" on the title page.

b. _____, Dell: 11838 ($1.75), 1977, paper.*
Reprinted 1978.*

c. _____, [French], Denoël: 238, 1977, paper.*
Translator: Françoise Cartano.

d. _____, Gollancz, London (£3.75), 1977.

e. _____, [Spanish], Editorial Bruguera: 12 (180 ptas), 1977, paper.*
Translator: Beatriz Podesta.

f. _____, [Italian], Libra Editrice, Bologna (L4000), 1977.*
Translator: Roberta Rambelli. Slan Libra 33. Introduction by "U.M."
[Ugo Malaguti].
Bound in green paper boards with gold lettering on the spine and
front cover.

g. _____, Sphere: 2964 (95p), 1978, paper.*

h. (DE GOD DER GRAMSCHAP) [Dutch], A W Bruna: SF 84, 1978, paper.*
Translator: Annemarie Kindt.

i. _____, Readers Union (British Book Club), Devon, 1978.*
Bound in gray paper boards with gold lettering on the spine. "1978" on
title page.

j. _____, Sphere: 2983 (95p), 1979, paper.

k. (DER GOTT DES ZORNS) [German], Bastei-Lubbe: 22006 (DM 4.80), 1979,
paper.*
Translator: Rosemarie Hundertmarck.

l. (   ) [Japanese], Sanrio, 1979, paper.

m. _____, Dell: 11838 ($2.25), 1980, paper.*

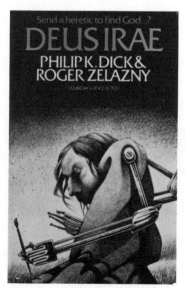

10.a.   10.e.   10.b.

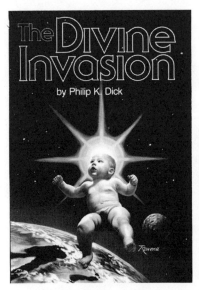

11.*a.*　　　　　　　10.*k.*　　　　　　　12.*p.*

11.　THE DIVINE INVASION

Manuscript title "VALIS REGAINED".
A sequel to VALIS.

**An air collision jeopardizes the successful conclusion of the Second
Coming. Emmanuel's Appolonian and Dionysian selves are divided by
partial amnesia. Their reintegration is opposed by Belial's forces of
decay, which control the Earth. The Paraclete's foster father, Herb
Asher, faces problems with his own redemption. Herb finds allies in the
prophet Elijah, his partner in a retail audio store; and in singer Linda
Fox, his own true love and a construct energized by VALIS. (Parts of
this novel coexist with the short story: "Chains of Air, Web of Aether.")**

a.　_____, Simon and Schuster, New York ($12.95), 1981.*
Three-piece binding, with royal blue cloth spine and light blue paper
boards with gold lettering on the spine. No date on the title page.
Printing code "10 9 8 7 6 5 4 3 2 1" on copyright page. A Timescape
Book.

12.　DO ANDROIDS DREAM OF ELECTRIC SHEEP?

Nominated for 1968 Nebula for Best Novel.

**Nexus-6 androids are almost human; a lack of empathy is their only
flaw. Eight of them flee Mars and hide among the citizens of the depop-
ulated San Francisco Bay Area. Rick Decard, a police bounty hunter,
must find and eliminate them. Difficulties arise because on a devastated
Earth all life is sacred to the followers of Wilbur Mercer, even sub-
normal chickenheads, electric animals and androids who believe themselves human.**

a. _____, Doubleday, Garden City ($3.95), 1968.*
Bound in gray cloth with gold lettering on the spine. "1968" on the title page. "FIRST EDITION" on the copyright page. Date code J5 (5th week of 1968) at lower right margin of page 210.

b. _____, Signet: T3800 ($0.75), 1969, paper.*

c. (TRAÜMEN ROBOTER VON ELEKTRISCHEN SCHAFEN?) [German], v. Schroder, Düsseldorf (DM 12.00), 1969, paper.*
Translator: Norbert Wolfl. Trade paperback size with a dustjacket.

d. (ANDROID WA DENKI HITSUJI NO YUME O MIRU KA?) [Japanese], Hayakawa Shobo: 3223 (Y330), 1969, paper.*
Translator: Asakura Hisashi. Issued in paper slipcase.

e. (DE ELEKTRISCHE NACHTMERRIE) [Dutch], Born: SF 13 (Fl 3.15), 1969, paper.*
Translator: Frankie Visser.

f. _____, Rapp & Whiting, London (21/-), 1969.

g. (TRAÜMAN ROBOTER VON ELEKTRISCHEN SCHAFEN?) [German], Heyne: 3273 (DM 2.80), 1971, paper.*
Translator: Norbert Wolfl.

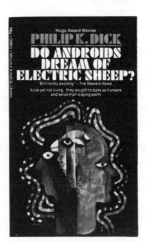

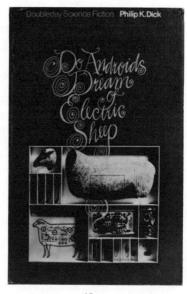

12.d.   12.b.   12.a.

h. _____, Signet: T4758 ($0.75), 1971, paper.*

i. (IL CACCIATORE DI ANDROIDI) [Italian], Galassia: 152 (L350), 1971, paper.
Translator: T Guasti.

j. _____, Panther: 03605 (30p), 1972, paper.*

k. (DROMMER ANDROIDER OM ELEKTRISKE FAR?) [Danish], Notabene, 1973, paper (?).
Translator: Jannick Storm.

l. (ANDROIDENS DROMMAR) [Swedish], Bernce, 1974, paper.
Translator: Roland Adlerberth.

m. (ROBOT-BLUES) [French], Champ Libre: 15, 1976, paper.

n. _____, Panther: 03605 (75p), 1977, paper.

o. (ANDROID WA DENKI HITSUJI NO YUME O MIRU KA?) [Japanese],
Hayakawa Shobo: SF 229 (Y330), 1977, paper.*

p. (DROMEN ANDROIDEN VAN ELEKTRISCHE SCHAPEN?) [Dutch],
Meulenhoff: SF 150, 1979, paper.*
Translator: Ivain Rodriguez de Leon. Apparently a second Dutch
translation.

q. (   ) [Hebrew], Massada.
Forthcoming, to be published in Israel.

r. _____, Ballantine.
Forthcoming. To be reprinted as a movie tie-in with photos from the
movie (see OTHER MEDIA section).

13. DR. BLOODMONEY, OR HOW WE GOT ALONG AFTER THE BOMB

Manuscript titles "In Earth's Diurnal Course", "A Terran Odyssey".
Nominated for 1965 Nebula for Best Novel.

**A post-nuclear war society struggles to reconstruct itself in an isolated
setting. Kept in contact with the outside world by an orbiting disc-
jockey, the group's members include Bill, an encysted telepathic twin;
Bruno Bluthgeld, the weapons expert responsible for the war; and Hoppy Harrington, a phocomelus who makes a frightening power play for
domination of the colony.**

a. _____, Ace: F-337 ($0.40), 1965, paper.*

13.a.   13.g.   13.k.

b. (CRONACHE DEL DOPOBOMBA) [Italian], Urania: 409 (L200), 1965, paper.
Translator: Ginetta Pignolo.

c. (OS SOBREVIVENTES) [Portuguese], Panorama: EP-A-3 (20$), 1967, paper.*
Translator: Maria Roque Casimiro.

d. (DR. BLUTHGELD, LEVEN NA DE BOM) [Dutch], Het Spectrum: Prisma 1382 (F 12.50), 1969, paper.*
Translator: Iet Houwer.

e. (DOCTEUR BLOODMONEY) [French], Opta, Paris (36.00F), 1970.*
Translator: Bruno Martin. Illustrated by Siudmak.
Combined with THE MAN IN THE HIGH CASTLE. Bound in blue cloth with silver lettering on the spine. Large logo stamped in silver on the front cover. Issued with clear plastic dustjacket.

f. (DR. BLOODMONEY) [French], J'ai Lu: 563, 1974, paper.*
Translator: Bruno Martin.

g. _____, Ace: 15670 ($1.50), 1976, paper.*

h. _____, Gregg Press, Boston ($11.00), 1977.*
Introduction by Norman Spinrad. Bound in dark green cloth with gold lettering on the spine. Title and author's name are on bright red background on the spine. "First Printing, June 1977" on the copyright page. Issued without dustjacket. Text is photo-reproduced from the 1965 Ace edition.

i. _____, Arrow: 914960 (80p), 1977, paper.*

j. (NACH DEM WELTUNTERGANG) [German], Goldmann: 0256 (DM 3.80), 1977, paper.*
Translator: Tony Westermayr.

k. _____, Dell, 11489 ($2.25), 1980, paper.*

14. DR. FUTURITY

(Expanded from "Time Pawn", Thrilling Wonder Stories, Summer 1954)
A time machine pulls a twenty-first century doctor four hundred years into the future. The science of medicine is then unknown because of a eugenics and voluntary euthanasia scheme. Parsons, the doctor, becomes involved in a complex time-hopping plot to change the course of the past by assassinating Sir Francis Drake.

a. _____, Ace: D-421 ($0.35), 1960, paper; with SLAVERS OF SPACE (John Brunner).*

b. (IL DOTTOR FUTURO) [Italian], Galassia: 30 (L180), 1963, paper.
Translator: L Pollini.

c. _____, Ace: 15697 ($0.95), 1972, paper; with THE UNTELEPORTED MAN (Dick).*

d. (LE VOYAGEUR DE L'INCONNU) [French], Le Masque: 2, 1974, paper. Translator: Florian Robinet.

e. _____, Methuen: 36540 (60p), 1976, paper.

f. _____, Magnum: 04610 (85p), 1979, paper.*

g. Berkley.
Purchased by Berkley but not yet scheduled.

 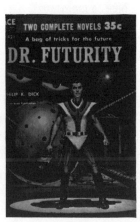 

14.*f.*   14.*a.*   14.*c.*

15. EYE IN THE SKY

Manuscript title "With Opened Mind".

Eight people are injured in a nuclear particle-beam accident. Miraculously alive, all of them begin to experience odd alterations in the ontologic fabric of existence. The survivors discover they are living in the objective dream worlds of the four most neurotic members of the group.

a. _____, Ace: D-211 ($0.35), 1957, paper.*

b. (L'OCCHIO NEL CIELO) [Italian], Urania: 201 (L150), 1959, paper.* Translator: Beata della Frattina.

c. (UCHU NO ME) [Japanese], Hayakawa Shobo: 3012 (Y200), 1959, paper.* Translator: Nakada Koji. Issued in paper slipcase.

d. (LES MONDES DIVERGENTS) [French], Editions Satellite (4.50NF), 1959, paper (?).

e. _____, Ace: H-39 ($0.60), 1968, paper.*

f. (OJET PA HIMLEN) [Danish], Hasselbalch (kr 9.85), 1968, paper (?). Translator: Niels Erik Wille.

g. (OJO CELESTE) [Spanish], Rumeu, 1969, paper.*
   Translator: Manuel Bartolome. Trade paperback size with front and back leaves folded over like a dustjacket.

h. (L'OCCHIO NEL CIELO) [Italian], Urania: 525 (L250), 1969, paper.*
   Translator: Beata della Frattina.

i. _____, Ace: 22385 ($0.60), 1970, paper.

j. (UND DIE ERDE STEHT STILL) [German], Goldmann: 0123 (DM 3.00), 1971, paper.*
   Translator: Hans-Ulrich Nichau. Reprinted 1975.

k. _____, Arrow: 005100 (30p), 1971, paper.*

l. (HET OOG AAN DE HEMEL) [Dutch], Luitingh: 2055 (Fl 3.95), 1972, paper.*
   Translator: Carl Lans.

m. _____, Ace: 22386 ($1.25), 1975, paper.*

n. (L'OEIL DANS LE CIEL) [French], Laffont (39.00F), 1976, paper.*
   Translator: Gerard Klein.

o. _____, Ace: 22387 ($1.50), 1977 (?), paper.*

p. _____, Arrow: 92760 (95p), 1979, paper.*

q. _____, Gregg Press, Boston ($14.95), 1979.*
   Introduction by Sandra Miesel. Frontispiece by Hannah Shapero. Bound in dark green cloth with gold lettering on the spine. Title and author's name are on bright red background on the spine. Author's signature stamped in gold on the front cover. "First Printing, November 1979" on the copyright page. Issued without dustjacket. Text is photo-reproduced from the 1957 Ace edition.

15.k.   15.a.   15.c.

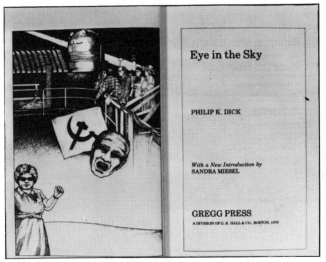

15.q. — *frontis and title page.*   15.p.

16. FLOW MY TEARS, THE POLICEMAN SAID

Nominated for 1975 Hugo for Best Novel.

Nominated for 1974 Nebula for Best Novel.

Won the 1975 John W Campbell Jr Award for Best Novel.

Experiments with a world-shifting drug draw Jason Taverner, a famous entertainer, into an alternate reality in which he is more than anonymous. Taverner is immediately harrassed by the police state organization of the new world. Taverner learns his displacement has been caused by Alys Buckman, the police commissioner's psychotic sister-lover, who is in love with him.

a. _____, Doubleday, Garden City ($6.95), 1974.*
Bound in rust colored cloth with silver lettering on the spine. Date code "O50" (50th week of 1973) at lower left margin of page 231. States "First edition" on the copyright page. This book was reprinted with a date code of "P7" (7th week of 1974) on page 231 and this printing was remaindered. The later printing leaves out the statement "First edition" on the copyright page—normal practice for Doubleday. Among the remaindered copies (which can be told by the splotched purple sprayed on the lower edges—the normal marking for a Doubleday remainder) were some first printings. "1974" on the title page of the first printing only. According to the author there were about 7500 copies of the first printing.

b. _____, Gollancz, London (£2.20), 1974.*
Bound in maroon paper boards with gold lettering on the spine. "1974" on the title page.

c. _____, DAW: 146 ($1.50), 1975, paper. Also numbered UW1166.*

d. (LE PRISME DU NEANT) [French], Le Masque: 22, 1975, paper.
Translator: Michel Deutsh.

e. _____, Readers Union (British Book Club), Devon, 1975.*
Bound in black paper boards with gold lettering on the spine. "1975"
on the title page.

f. _____, DAW: UW1266 ($1.50), 1976, paper.*

g. _____, Panther: 04203 (60p), 1976, paper.*

h. (FLUYAN MIS LAGRIMAS, DIJO EL POLICIA) [Spanish], Ediciones
Acervo, Barcelona, 1976.*
Translator: Domingo Santos.
Bound in blue paper boards with silver lettering on the spine and front
cover. Has a small (about 1½ inch high) yellow banner wrapped
around the dustjacket, and a clear plastic wrapper around them both.

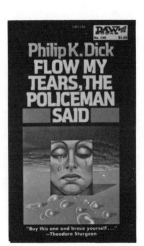

16.c.

16.h.

16.i.

i. (EINE ANDERE WELT) [German], Heyne: 3528 (DM 4.80), 1977, paper.*
Translator: Walter Brumm.

j. (EPISODIO TEMPORALE) [Italian], Nord (L3000), 1977, paper.*
Translator: Roberta Rambelli. Narrativa D'Anticipazione 8. Introduction by Valerio Fissone. About the size of an American hardcover.

k. _____, Panther: 04203 (80p), 1979, paper.*

l. (   ) [Japanese], Sanrio, 1979, paper.

m. _____, DAW: 438 ($2.25), 1981, paper. Also numbered UE1624.*

n. (   ) [Hebrew], Massada.
Forthcoming, to be published in Israel.

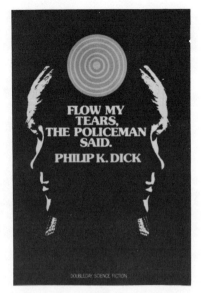

16.a.

16.j.

17. GALACTIC POT-HEALER

Manuscript title "The Glimmung of Plowman's Planet".

The Glimmung, an alien with supernatural powers, has assembled several demoralized groups of artisans to aid in the restoration of a mystical sunken cathedral. The cathedral is surrounded by ontological and epistemological symbols and events, and is guarded by an evil anti-Glimmung.

a. _____, Berkley: X1705 ($0.60), 1969, paper.*

b. _____, Science Fiction Book Club, Garden City, 1970.*
Bound in black paper boards with gray lettering on the spine. Date code 08L at lower left margin of page 145. No date on the title page.

c. _____, Gollancz, London (£1.60), 1971.*
Bound in maroon paper boards with gold lettering on the spine. "1971" on the title page.

d. _____, Pan: 23337 (25p), 1972, paper.*

e. _____, Berkley: 02569 ($0.95), 1974, paper.*

f. (JOE VON DER MILCHSTRASSE) [German], Fischer Orbit: FO-10, 1974, paper.*
Translator: Joachim Pente.

g. _____, Pan: 23337 (60p), 1977, paper.

17.*a*.   17.*d*.   17.*f*.

h. (MANQUE DE POT!) [French], Champ Libre: 19, 1977, paper.

i. (DE POTTENGENEZER VAN DE MELKWEG) [Dutch], Scala: 621, 1977, paper.*
Translator: R Neehus.

j. (GIU' NELLA CATTEDRALE) [Italian], Galassia: 235 (L2000), 1979, paper.
Translator: P Anselmi.

17.*i*.   17.*b*.

18. THE GAME-PLAYERS OF TITAN

The human remnants of the intersystem wars play a territory-oriented game designed to maximize births in an almost sterile population. Pete Garden, with the assistance of some Psis, determines that the Titanian vugs are horning in on the game, and that an even more radical faction of the vugs wants to sterilize Terra entirely.

a. _____, Ace: F-251 ($0.40), 1963, paper.*

b. (TORNEO MORTAL) [Spanish], Nebula: 106, 1965, paper.*
   Translator: Francisco Carzorla Olmo.

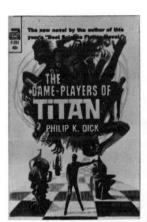  

18.a.   18.b.   18.j.

c. (I GIOCATORI DI TITANO) [Italian], Galassia: 73 (L300), 1966, paper.
   Translator: L Morelli.

d. _____, Sphere: 2957 (5/-), 1969, paper.

e. _____, Ace: 27310 ($0.75), 1972, paper.*

f. _____, Sphere: 2959 (30p), 1973, paper.

g. (DE SPELERS VAN TITAN) [Dutch], Meulenhoff: SF 71, 1973, paper.*
   Translator: David Markus.

h. _____, White Lion, London (£1.80), 1974.*
   Bound in dark blue paper boards with gold lettering stamped on the spine. States "White Lion edition, 1974" on copyright page and otherwise makes no indication of edition or printing. Name on spine is "R.A. Dick" (the author of THE GHOST AND MRS. MUIR). No date on the title page.

i. _____, Sphere: 2961 (65p), 1977, paper.
   Reprinted 1978.

j. (LES JOUEURS DE TITAN) [French], La Masque: 74, 1978, paper.*
Translator: Maxime Barriere.

k. (DAS GLOBUS-SPIEL) [German], Goldmann: 23272 (DM 4.80), 1978, paper.*
Translator: Tony Westermayr.

l. _____, Gregg Press, Boston ($13.95), 1979.*
Introduction by Robert Thurston. Frontispiece by Hannah Shapero. Bound in dark green cloth with gold lettering on the spine. Title and author's name are on bright red background on the spine. Author's signature stamped in gold on the front cover. "First Printing, April 1979" on the copyright page. Issued without dustjacket. Text is photo-reproduced from the 1963 Ace edition.

m. (   ) [Hebrew], Massada.
Forthcoming, to be published in Israel.

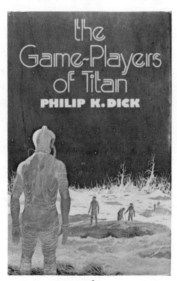

18.h.

18.g.

19. THE GANYMEDE TAKEOVER

(with Ray Nelson)

The worm-like, telepathic Ganymedeans have conquered and are now beginning to occupy the Earth. Pockets of resistance are forming, chief among them in the Bale of Tennessee. News reporters, dissident black separatists and former world government psychologists are uniting there to sabotage, suborn and defeat the Ganymedeans and Earth's own reactionary elements.

a. _____, Ace: G-637 ($0.50), 1967, paper.*

b. (L'ORA DEI GRANDI VERMI) [Italian], Urania: 479 (L250), 1968, paper.*
   Translator: Luciana Agnoli Zucchini.

c. _____, Arrow: B537 (25p), 1971, paper.*

d. (DIE INVASOREN VON GANYMED) [German], Bergisch Gladbach: 21082, 1976, paper.
   Translator: Bernt Kling.

e. _____, Ace: 27346 ($1.50), 1977, paper.*

f. (L'ORA DEI GRANDI VERMI) [Italian], Urania: 808 (L900), 1979, paper.*
   Translator: Luciana Agnoli Zucchini.

g. _____, Arrow: 5370 (95p), 1980, paper.

19.f.   19.a.   20.a.

20. THE GOLDEN MAN
   Edited by Mark Hurst.
   Introduction, Story Notes and Afterword by Philip K Dick.
   Foreword by Mark Hurst.
   Contents: The Golden Man; Return Match; The King Of The Elves; The Mold Of Yancy; Not By Its Cover; The Little Black Box; The Unreconstructed M; The War With The Fnools; The Last Of The Masters; Meddler; A Game Of Unchance; Sales Pitch; Precious Artifact; Small Town; The Pre-Persons.

a. _____, Berkley: 04288 ($2.25), 1980, paper.*

b. _____, Science Fiction Book Club, Garden City, 1981.*
   Bound in gold paper boards with purple lettering on the spine.

Publisher name Berkley appears on the spine. No date on the title
page. Date code K27 on page 325.

c.   _____, Methuen, 1981, paper.
Forthcoming.

21.   A HANDFUL OF DARKNESS

Contents: Colony; Impostor; Expendable; Planet For Transients; Prominent Author; The Builder; The Little Movement; The Preserving Machine; The Impossible Planet; The Indefatigable Frog;
The Turning Wheel; Progeny; Upon The Dull Earth; The
Cookie Lady; Exhibit Piece.

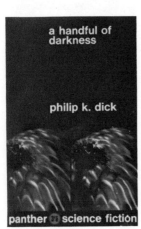      

21.c.   21.a.   22.a.

a.   _____, Rich & Cowan, London (10/6), 1955.*
Bound in dark blue paper boards with silver lettering and spaceship
logo on the spine. States "First Published—1955" on the copyright page
with no other indications of editions or printings. No date on the title
page. According to L W Currey there is a second binding state with
orange paper boards with black lettering on the spine. The compiler
saw a third state consisting of very heavy orange boards with black lettering on the spine, but the spaceship logo had been replaced by the
publisher's logo (a stylized lion) on the spine. It is not known if this
was issued by the publisher or was privately rebound from the second
binding state. The latter case is more likely. Also, according to L W
Currey there exists a later dustjacket state listing Dick's WORLD OF
CHANCE, which has been observed on both of the first two binding
states. Currey indicates that the blue binding has priority.

b. (EINE HANDVOLL DUNKELHEIT) [German], Terra Sonderband: 76, 1963, paper.
Abridged.

c. _____, Panther: 2108 (3/6), 1966, paper.*
Omits: The Little Movement and The Preserving Machine.

d. (EEN HANDVOL DUISTERNIS) [Dutch], A W Bruna: 1100 (Fl 2.50), 1968, paper.*
Translator: Henk Bouwman.
Contains only Colony; Impostor; Expendable; Planet For Transients; The Builder; The Impossible Planet; Progeny; Upon The Dull Earth; and The Cookie Lady from the original collection. It also adds the story Second Variety.

e. (EN HANDFULD MORKE) [Danish], Stig Vendelkaer, 1973, paper (?).
Translator: Kristian Kliim.

f. (PHILIP K. DICK OMNIBUS) [Dutch], A W Bruna: SF 68, 1977, paper.
Combines the Dutch edition of A HANDFUL OF DARKNESS (see d. above) with the original Dutch collection EEN SWIBBEL VOOR DAG EN NACHT.

g. _____, Gregg Press, Boston ($11.00), 1978.*
Introduction by Richard A Lupoff. Frontispiece by Hannah Shapero. Bound in dark green cloth with gold lettering on the spine. Title and author's name are on bright red background on the spine. "First Printing, June 1978" on the copyright page. Issued without dustjacket. Text is photo-reproduced from the 1955 Rich & Cowan edition.

h. _____, Panther: 04804 (95p), 1980, paper.

LIES, INC.
See THE UNTELEPORTED MAN

22. **LE LIVRE D'OR DE LA SCIENCE-FICTION PHILIP K. DICK**
Edited by Marcel Thaon.
Contents: Labyrinthe De Mort (Preface by Marcel Thaon); Pay For The Printer; The Impossible Planet; Human Is; Small Town; The Commuter; A Game Of Unchance; Shell Game; Recall Mechanism; Misadjustment; Your Appointment Will Be Yesterday; Stand-By; The Days Of Perky Pat; Bibliography of Philip K. Dick.

a. _____, Presses Pocket: 5051, 1979, paper.*
All stories translated by Marcel Thaon.

23. THE MAN IN THE HIGH CASTLE

Won the 1963 Hugo for Best Novel.

The Axis powers have won the Second World War. Japan and Germany have divided and occupied the United States. One man, Hawthorne Abendsen, has correctly divined an alternate existence and he serves as a rallying post for dissident Americans and a target for Nazi exterminators. The Nazis have a plan for exterminating the rest of non-Aryan humanity too, involving a putative Swedish diplomat named Baynes and Mr. N. Tagomi, a mild-mannered trade attaché in occupied San Francisco.

a. _____, Putnam, New York ($3.95), 1962.*
   Bound in black cloth with red lettering on the front cover and spine. Date code "D36" (36th week, 1962) on lower left margin of page 239. Top edges stained yellow. No date on the title page. (Putnam normally does not mark first printings, but explicitly marks later printings.)

b. _____, Science Fiction Book Club, Garden City, 1962.*
   Bound in black paper boards with orange lettering on the front cover and the spine. Top edges stained orange. No indication of edition or printing. Date code "D45" on lower left margin of page 239.

23.a.   23.s.

c. _____, Popular: SP250 ($0.50), 1964, paper.

d. (TAKAI SHIRO NO OTOKO) [Japanese], Hayakawa Shobo (Y360), 1965, paper.*
   Translator: Kawaguchi Shokichi. Issued in paper slipcase.

e. (LA SVASTICA SUL SOLE) [Italian], La Tribuna (Science Fiction Book Club): 15 (L2000), 1965, paper.
Translator: Romolo Minelli.

f. _____, Penguin: 2376 (5/-), 1965, paper.*

g. _____, Popular: 60-2289 ($0.60), 1968, paper.*

h. (LAARZEN IN DE NACHT) [Dutch], Born: SF 4 (Fl 2.95), 1968, paper.*
Translator: Ben Dull.

i. (LE MAÎTRE DU HAUT CHATEAU) [French], Opta, Paris (36.00F), 1970.*
Translator: Jacques Parsons. Illustrated by Siudmak.
Combined with DR. BLOODMONEY. Bound in blue cloth with silver lettering on the spine. Large logo stamped in silver on the front cover. Issued with clear plastic dustjacket.

j. (MANDEN I DEN STORE FAESTNING) [Danish], Stig Vendelkaer, 1973, paper.
Translator: Jorgen Bech-Jessen.

23.d.   23.m.   23.f.

k. (DAS ORAKEL VOM BERGE) [German], Konig: SF 34 (DM 4.80), 1973, paper.*
Translator: Heinz Nagel.

l. _____, Berkley: 02543 ($1.25), 1974, paper.*

m. (EL HOMBRE EN EL CASTILLO) [Spanish], Minotauro, Buenos Aires, 1974, paper.*
Translator: Manuel Figueroa. Published in Argentina.
There was apparently another edition of this book from another

Argentinian publisher in the 1960s. It was trade paperback size and used four styles of type—all in all a very nice edition. Interestingly, ads in this book indicated that the only other books available from the publisher were books proselytizing the Cuban revolution. Dick's copy of this book was stolen, so no further information is available.

n. (LE MAÎTRE DU HAUT CHATEAU) [French], J'ai Lu: 567, 1974, paper. Translator: Jacques Parsons.

o. _____, Gollancz, London (£2.40), 1975.*
Bound in blue paper boards with gold lettering on the spine. "1975" on the title page.

  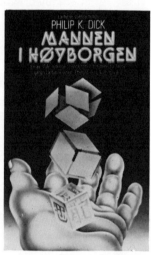

23.c.   23.p.   23.r.

p. _____, Penguin: 2376 (60p), 1976, paper.*

q. _____, Readers Union (British), Devon, 1976.*
Bound in dark red paper with gold lettering on the spine.

r. (MANNEN I HOYBORGEN) [Norwegian], Lanterne: L362, 1977, paper.* Translator: Peter Haars.

s. (LA SVASTICA SUL SOLE) [Italian], Nord, Milan (L3500), 1977.*
Translator: Roberta Rambelli. Introduction by Carlo Pagetti.
Cosmo Classici Della Fantascienza 29.
Bound in blue paper boards with white lettering on the spine.

t. _____, Berkley: 03908 ($1.75), 1978, paper.*

u. _____, Penguin: 2376 (75p), 1978, paper.*

v. _____, Gregg Press, Boston ($9.95), 1979.*
Introduction by Joseph Milicia. Frontispiece by Hannah Shapero.
Bound in dark green cloth with gold lettering on the spine. Title and

author's name are on bright red background on the spine. Author's signature stamped in gold on the front cover. "First Printing, April 1979" on the copyright page. Issued without dustjacket. Text is photo-reproduced from the 1962 Putnam edition.

w. (DE MAN IN HET HOGE KASTEEL) [Dutch], Elsevier, 1979, paper.*
   Translators: Ben Dull and Ruud Bal.

x. (   ) [Greek], Exantas, 1979 (?), paper (?).

y. (   ) [Polish], Czytelnik, 1979 (?), paper (?).

z. _____, Berkley: 04323 ($1.95), 1979, paper.*

aa. (DAS ORAKEL VOM BERGE) [German], Bastei-Lubbe: 22021 (DM 5.80), 1980, paper.*
   Translator: Heinz Nagel.

ab. _____, Berkley: 05051 ($2.25), 1981, paper.*

ac. (   ) [Hebrew], Massada.
   Forthcoming, to be published in Israel.

This title has now been translated into eleven different languages; more than any other of Dick's titles. And it is entirely possible that some translations have been missed.

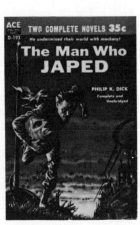

23.*w.*   24.*a.*   24.*f.*

24. THE MAN WHO JAPED

Earth is in the repressive grip of Morec—Moral Reclamation—a spying, hereditary government. The only alternatives to its strict control are emigration or psychotherapy. Allen Purcell is one of the leaders of Morec; a man who designs ethical propaganda for the edification of the citizens. Without realizing the symbology behind his actions, Purcell has defaced the statue of Major Streeter, the central figure of Morec. It is not clear to Purcell whether his deeds mean revolution or insanity.

a. _____, Ace: D-193 ($0.35), 1956, paper; with THE SPACE-BORN (E C Tubb).*

b. (PLANETAS MORALES) [Spanish], Cenit: 6, 1960, paper.

c. (REDENZIONE IMMORALE) [Italian], Galassia: 43 (L300), 1964, paper. Translator: L Morelli.

d. _____, Ace: 51910 ($0.95), 1973, paper.*

e. (LE DETOURNEUR) [French], Sagittaire: 8, 1977, paper.* Translators: Phillippe Lorrain and Baudouin Panloup.

f. _____, Eyre Methuen, London (£3.50), 1978.* Bound in green paper boards with gold lettering on the spine. "First published in Great Britain 1978" on the copyright page. The book is small—about paperback size.

g. _____, Magnum: 02590 (85p), 1978, paper.* Reprinted 1980.

25. MARTIAN TIME-SLIP

("All We Marsmen", Worlds of Tomorrow, sr3, Aug 1963)

Expanded from the magazine version.

The unions control Mars, the colonial world of speculation, and Arnie Kott the plumber is at the top of the heap. Arnie wants to use the time-warping abilities of Manfred, a schizophrenic child, to control Martian real estate. Kott sets Jack Bolen the task of building a machine to communicate with Manfred. Instead, Manfred catches them up in a degenerating time-loop, fearing the vision of his own future. Only the Martians can communicate telepathically with Manfred and aid him in escaping from a future that is gradually spreading back to obliterate the past.

a. _____, Ballantine: U2191 ($0.50), 1964, paper.*

b. (KASEI NO TIME SLIP) [Japanese], Hayakawa Shobo: 3129 (Y350), 1966, paper.* Translator: Obi Fusa. Issued in paper slipcase.

c. (MOZART FÜR MARSIANER) [German], Insel Verlag, Frankfurt, 1973.* Translator: Renate Laux. Bound in purple paper boards with silver lettering on the spine. Text printed in purple ink.

d. (NOI MARZIANI) [Italian], Nord, Milan (L1500), 1974.

e. (MARTIAANSE TIJDSVERSCHUIVING) [Dutch], Meulenhoff: SF 79, paper.* Translator: Parma van Loon.

f. _____, NEL, London (£3.95), 1976.* Bound in blue paper boards with gold lettering on the spine and front cover. "This edition first published in Great Britain by // New English Library, // . . . in 1976" on the copyright page. Introduction by Brian W Aldiss.

g. _____, Ballantine: 25224 ($1.50), 1976, paper.*

h. _____, NEL: 30016 (90p), 1977, paper.*

i. (   ) [Swedish], Kindbergs, 1978 (?), paper.

j. (TIEMPO DE MARTE) [Spanish], Nebulae: 18, 1979, paper.*
Translator: Norma B de Lopez. Published in Argentina.

k. _____, Ballantine: 29560 ($2.25), 1981, paper.*
A Del Rey Book.

25.e.

25.a.

25.c.

26. A MAZE OF DEATH

A disgruntled group of misfits is moved to an experimental planet after personal contact with their transcendant deity. Though Delmak-0 is supposed to be uninhabited, the colonists begin to suffer frequent and unusual deaths. Upon infiltration of a hidden building, they discover they are guinea pigs in a long range experiment, and that they themselves are the experimenters.

a. _____, Doubleday, Garden City ($4.95), 1970.*
Bound in royal blue cloth with silver lettering on the spine. "1970" on the title page. "First Edition" on the copyright page. Date code "L21" at the lower right margin of page 216. According to David Hartwell this book was accidently pulped, leaving only library and review copies actually distributed.

b. _____, Paperback Library: 64-636 ($0.75), 1971, paper.*
Reprinted.

c.   _____, Gollancz, London (£1.80), 1972.*
Bound in maroon paper boards with gold lettering stamped on the spine. "1972" on the title page. States nothing about printing or edition on the copyright page (normal practice for Gollancz; however, they generally mark later printings).

d.   (VLUCHT IN VISIONEN) [Dutch], Het Spectrum: Prisma 1517 (Fl 3.00), 1972, paper.
Translator: Suurmeijer.

e.   (AU BOUT DU LABYRINTHE) [French], Laffont, 1972, paper (?).
Translator: Alain Doremieux.

25.h.

26.k.

26.a.

f.   _____, Pan: 23769 (35p), 1973, paper.*

g.   (IRRGARTEN DES TODES) [German], Heyne: 3397, 1974, paper.
Translator: Yoma Cap.

h.   (LABIRINTO DI MORTE) [Italian], La Tribuna (Science Fiction Book Club): 46 (L1500), 1974, paper.
Translator: V Curtoni.

i.   _____, Pan: 23769 (60p), 1977, paper.

j.   (AU BOUT DU LABYINTHE) [French], J'ai Lu: 774, 1977, paper.*
Translator: Alain Doremieux.

k.   _____, Bantam: 10740 ($1.75), 1977, paper.*

l.   (   ) [Japanese], Sanrio: 3-B (Y380), 1979, paper.*

26.b.   26.f.

27. MILLEMONDINVERNO 1975: TRE ROMANZI COMPLETI DI PHILIP K. DICK

Italian collection.

Contents: Dr. Bloodmoney, Or How We Got Along After The Bomb; A Glass Of Darkness; Time Out Of Joint.

a. _____, Mondadori: Supplemento A Urania 684 (L1500), 1975, paper.*

27.a.   28.a.

28. NOW WAIT FOR LAST YEAR

Eric Sweetscent is a brilliant surgeon with a psychotic wife. He is co-opted into preserving the life of Earth's strongman, Gino Molinari. Molinari is directing Earth's efforts in the Proxman-Reeg interstellar war. Earth has entered the struggle on the side of the Proxmen, who appear to be losing the moral conflict as well as the war. JJ-180, a deadly and addictive drug, propels Sweetscent and Molinari through time and alternate continuums in attempts to find options to the Proxmen's domination of the Earth.

28.f.   28.c.   28.g.

a. _____, Doubleday, Garden City ($3.95), 1966.*
Bound in charcoal black cloth with gold lettering on the spine. "1966" on the title page. "First Edition" on the copyright page. Date code H9 (9th week of 1966) at the lower right margin of page 214.

b. (EN ATTENDANT L'ANNÉE DERNIÈRE) [French], Opta, Paris (31.00F), 1968.*
Translator: Michel Deutsh. Introduction by John Brunner.
Illustrated. Combined with COUNTER-CLOCK WORLD. Bound in green cloth with gold lettering on the spine. Large logo stamped in gold on the front cover. Dick's copy has no dustjacket.

c. _____, Macfadden: 60-352 ($0.60), 1968, paper.*

d. (ILLUSIONE DI POTERE) [Italian], Nord, Milan, (L1000), 1971.*
Cosmo Collana Di Fantascienza 12.
Translator: Gabriele Tamburini. Bound in silver paper boards with black lettering on the spine.

e. _____, Manor: 12214 ($1.25), 1974, paper.*
Also contains "Epigram" by Tessa B. Dick (?).

f. _____, Panther: 04208 (50p), 1975, paper.*
Reprinted 1976.

g. (WACHT NU OP VORIG JAAR) [Dutch], Meulenhoff: SF 106, 1976, paper.*
Translator: Roderick Lennaert van Rhyn.

h. _____, Manor: 12410 ($1.25), 1976, paper.*
Also contains "Epigram" by Tessa B. Dick.

i. (EN ATTENDANT L'ANNÉE DERNIÈRE) [French], La Livre de Poche, 1977, paper.

j. _____, Panther: 04208 (85p), 1979, paper.

A Science Fiction Book Club edition was announced for Feb 1968 (item #1210). However, no one the compiler contacted has ever seen a copy. There is some speculation that the announcement was an attempt to remainder the first edition, a practice Doubleday apparently later used for some other books (the Science Fiction Book Club is actually a part of Doubleday and has been throughout the Club's existence).

29. DE ONMOGELIJKE PLANEET

Dutch collection.
Contents: The Impossible Planet; Impostor; Roog; Pay For The Printer; War Veteran; Beyond Lies The Wub; The Crawlers; Captive Market; Colony.

a. _____, A W Bruna: SF 40, 1976, paper.*
Translators: Henk Bouwman—The Impossible Planet; Impostor; Colony.
Amos Baat—all others.

29.a.

30.b.

30. OUR FRIENDS FROM FROLIX 8

Super-intelligent New Men led by Amos Ild and telepathic Unusuals led by Willis Gram alternate control of Earth's government. When Nick Appleton, selected as a random representative of the Normals, shows signs of rebellion and discontent, Gram orders action against the followers of Thors Provoni, the spiritual leader of the Normals. Provoni is even at that moment returning from an interstellar voyage with some powerful extraterrestrial allies from the Frolixian System.

a. _____, Ace: 64400 ($0.60), 1970, paper.*

b. _____, Science Fiction Book Club, Garden City, 1971.*
Bound in rust brown paper boards with black lettering on the spine. "Ace Books" on spine. Date code B3 (3rd week of 1971) at lower right margin of page 184.

c. (I NOSTRI AMICI DI FROLIX 8) [Italian], Galassia: 166, (L400), 1971, paper.
Translator: R Rambelli.

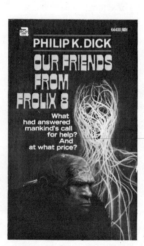

30.e.   30.a.   30.g.

d. (MESSAGE DE FROLIX 8) [French], Opta, 1972, paper (?).
Translator: Robert Louit.

e. _____, Panther: 04295 (60p), 1976, paper.*
Reprinted 1976.

f. _____, Ace: 64401 ($1.50), 1977, paper.*

g. (DIE MEHRBEGABTEN) [German], Goldmann: 23275 (DM 5.80), 1978, paper.*
Translator: Tony Westermayr.

h. (ONZE VRIENDEN VAN FROLIX 8) [Dutch], Meulenhoff: SF 118, 1977, paper.*
Translator: Jaime Martijn.

i. (MESSAGE DE FROLIX 8) [French], Le Masque: 83, 1978, paper.
Translator: Robert Louit.

31. THE OWL IN DAYLIGHT

a. _____, Simon and Schuster.
Forthcoming.

32. THE PENULTIMATE TRUTH

Most humans live in tank cities far below the surface of the Earth, believing themselves to be safe from the ongoing nuclear war above their heads. In fact, the war has been over for ten years, and instead of a radioactive ruin, the planet is a vast park, ruled by feudal barons who are playing power politics with the buried masses of their fellow men.

a. _____, Belmont: 92-603 ($0.50), 1964, paper.*

b. (LA PENULTIMA VERITA) [Italian], Science Fiction Book Club, La Tribuna: 12 (L600), 1966, paper.*
Translator: Mauro Cesari.
Paperback with stiff covers and with the front and back covers folded over as in a dustjacket.

c. _____, Cape, London (25/-), 1967.*
Bound in purple paper boards with silver lettering on the spine. No date on the title page. "First published in Great Britain 1967" on the copyright page.

d. _____, Penguin: 003105 (30p, 6/-), 1970, paper.

e. (ZEHN JAHRE NACH DEM BLITZ) [German], Goldmann: 0112 (DM 2.80), 1970, paper.*
Translator: Tony Westermayr.

f. (HET UUR DER WAARHEID) [Dutch], Meulenhoff: SF 49 (Fl 4.25), 1971, paper.*
Translator. F Lancel.

g. (LA VÉRITÉ AVANT-DERNIÈRE) [French], Laffont, 1974, paper.*
Translator: Alain Doremieux.

h. (ZEHN JAHRE NACH DEM BLITZ) [German], Goldmann: 0112, 1975, paper.*
Translator: Tony Westermayr.

i. _____, Leisure Books: 285NK ($0.95), 1975, paper.

j. (LA PENULTIMA VERDAD) [Spanish], Martinez Roca: SF 2, 1976, paper.*
Translator: Antonio Ribera.

k. _____, Panther: 04787 (95p), 1978, paper.*

l. (LA VÉRITÉ AVANT-DERNIÈRE) [French], J'ai Lu: 910, 1979, paper.*
Translator: Alain Doremieux.

m. _____, Dell: 16926 ($1.95), 1980, paper.*

32.j.

32.c.

32.a.

32.m.

33. A PHILIP K. DICK OMNIBUS

Contents: The Crack In Space; The Unteleported Man; Dr. Futurity.

a. _____, Sidgwick & Jackson, London (39/-, £1.95), 1970.*
Bound in blue paper boards with silver lettering on the spine. No date
on the title page. "This omnibus edition copyright © 1970 by //
Sidgwick and Jackson Limited" on the copyright page.

34. THE PRESERVING MACHINE

Contents: The Preserving Machine; War Game; Upon The Dull Earth;
Roog; War Veteran; Top Stand-By Job; Beyond Lies The Wub;
We Can Remember It For You Wholesale; Captive Market; If
There Were No Benny Cemoli; Retreat Syndrome; The
Crawlers; Oh, To Be A Blobel!; What The Dead Men Say; Pay
For The Printer.

  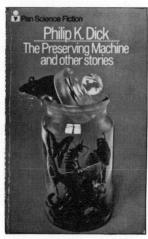

34.a.   34.b.   34.d.

a. _____, Ace: 67800 ($0.95), 1969, paper.*

b. _____, Science Fiction Book Club, Garden City, 1970.*
Bound in gray paper boards with green lettering on the spine. Ace
Books logo on the spine. Top edges stained green. Date code 48K (48th
week of 1969) at lower left margin of page 309.

c. _____, Gollancz, London (£1.60), 1971.*
Omits: What The Dead Men Say.
Bound in maroon paper boards with gold lettering on the spine. "1971"
on the title page.

d. _____, Pan: 23363 (35p), 1972, paper.*

e. _____, Ace: 67801 ($1.95), 1976, paper.*

f. (LE VOCI DI DOPO) [Italian], Fanucci: Futuro 26 (L4500), 1976, paper.*
Translator: M Nati.
Omits: We Can Remember It For You Wholesale; Retreat Syndrome;
and Oh, To Be A Blobel!. Adds the article "Philip K. Dick & The Umbrella Of Light" by Angus Taylor.

g. _____, Pan: 23363 (70p), 1977, paper.*

h. (LA MAQUINA PRESERVADORA) [Spanish], Edhasa: 23, 1978 (?), paper.
Translator: Norma Barrios de Lopez.
Contains: The Preserving Machine; War Game; Roog; War Veteran;
Top Stand-By Job; Beyond Lies The Wub; We Can Remember It For
You Wholesale; and If There Were No Benny Cemoli.

i. (EN LA TIERRA SOMBRIA) [Spanish], Edhasa: 26, 1978, paper.*
Translator: Norma Barrios de Lopez.
Contains: Upon The Dull Earth; Captive Market; Retreat Syndrome;
The Crawlers; Oh, To Be A Blobel!; What the Dead Men Say; and Pay
For The Printer.

j. (LA MAQUINA PRESERVADORA) [Spanish], Nebulae: 22, 1979, paper.*
Published in Argentina.

35.   LE RETOUR DES EXPLORATEURS

("Explorers We", Fantasy & Science Fiction, Jan 1959)
French.

a. _____, L'Aube Enclavée, Sept 1977, paper.*
Translator: Pierre Billon.
Limited edition booklet put out at the 2nd Festival International de la
Science-Fiction de Metz, 19-25 September 1977.

36.   A SCANNER DARKLY

Won the 1979 Graouilly d'Or Award for Best Novel (presented at the
Festival de Metz in France).
**Bob Arctor leads a double life. As a drug-pusher, he is killing his
friends and himself with Substance D. D means death. In his other per-
sona, Bob is a narcotics agent named Fred who is hot on the trail of a
pusher by the name of Bob Arctor.**

35.a.

36.a.

a. _____, Doubleday, Garden City ($6.95), 1977.*
Bound in beige paper boards with black lettering on the spine. Date code "G51" (51st week, 1976) appears on the lower right margin of page 216. "1977" on the title page. States "First Edition" on the copyright page.

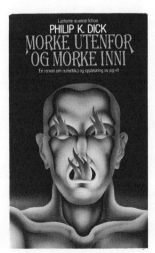

36.i.

36.h.

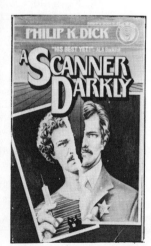

36.d.

b. _____, Science Fiction Book Club, Garden City, 1977.*
Date code H05 on page 216.

c. _____, Gollancz, London (£3.50), 1977.*
Bound in blue paper boards with gold lettering on the spine. "1977" on the title page.

d. _____, Ballantine: 26064 ($1.95), 1977, paper.*

e. _____, Science Fiction Book Club (British), London, 1978.

f. _____, Panther: 04553 (95p), 1978, paper.*

g. (SUBSTANCE MORT) [French], Denoël: 252, 1978, paper.*
Translator: Robert Louit.

h. (SCRUTARE NEL BUIO) [Italian], Nord (L3500), 1979, paper.*
Translators: Valerio Fissore and Sandro Pergameno.
Introduction by Valerio Fissore. Narrativa D'Anticipazione 15.

i. (MORKE UTENFOR OG MORKE INNI) [Norwegian], Gyldendal Norsk Forlag: L435, 1979, paper.*
Translator: Peter Haars.

j. (   ) [Japanese], Sanrio, 1979, paper.

k. (SCHIMMIGE BEELDEN) [Dutch], Bruna, 1979, paper (?).

37. THE SIMULACRA

A vivacious young woman named Nicole Thibodeaux has for seventy-three years been running the United States as the president's wife. Nicole's husbands are manufactured by a German instrument company associated with a drug cartel which has just managed to obtain the president's order banning psychoanalysis. One psychoanalyst, Dr. Egon Superb, is left in practice because he happens to be treating Nicole's favorite entertainers. (Parts of this incredibly complex novel first appeared as the short story: "Novelty Act.")

a. _____, Ace: F-301 ($0.40), 1964, paper.*

b. (I SIMULACRI) [Italian], Science Fiction Book Club, La Tribuna: 6 (L600), 1965, paper.*
Translator: Romolo Minelli.
Paperback with stiff covers and with the front and back covers folded over as in a dustjacket.

c. (SIMULACRES) [French], Calmann-Levy, 1973, paper.*
Translators: Marcel Thaon and Christian Gueret.

d. (SIMULACRES) [French], J'ai Lu: 594, 1975, paper.*
Translators: Marcel Thaon and Christian Gueret.

e. _____, Ace: 76701 ($1.50), 1976, paper.*

f. _____, Eyre Methuen, London (£2.95), 1977.*
Bound in black paper boards with silver lettering on the spine. No date on the title page. "First published in Great Britain 1977 by Eyre Methuen Ltd." on the copyright page. This book is small—about paperback size.

g. _____, Magnum: 01970 (75p), 1977, paper.

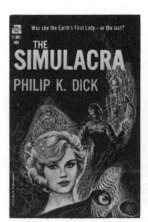

37.*a*.   37.*h*.   37.*f*.

h. (SIMULACRA) [German], Knaur SF: 708 (DM 5.80), 1978, paper.*
Translator: Uwe Anton.

i. (I SIMULACRI) [Italian], Nord, Milan, 1980.
Cosmo Classici Della Fantascienza 42.

j. (   ) [Hebrew], Massada.
Forthcoming, to be published in Israel.

38. SOLAR LOTTERY

SOLAR LOTTERY version differs considerably from WORLD OF CHANCE version. Ace wanted revisions and Rich & Cowan wanted revisions, both different, so the author satisfied them both.

Anyone may become world director by the random selection of his power card within a magnetic bottle. Most people have sold their power cards and thus placed themselves in thrall to the powerful feudal economic barons. A renegade politician with his eyes on the stars becomes director, and the deposed feudal baron attempts his assassination with the aid of a pseudo-human construct.

a. _____, Ace: D-103, ($0.35), 1955, paper; with THE BIG JUMP (Leigh Brackett).*

b. (as WORLD OF CHANCE), Rich & Cowan, London (9/6), 1956.*
Bound in blue paper boards with silver lettering and spaceship logo on the spine. "First published 1956" on the copyright page. No date on the title page. Tim Underwood has seen a copy bound in green cloth with heavy boards and a metal eyelet at the top end of the spine. It is not known if this was a library edition from the publisher or a privately rebound copy.

38.b.

38.c.

c. (as WORLD OF CHANCE), Science Fiction Book Club (British), London, 1957.*
Book Club Series No. 26. Bound in peacock blue paper boards with blue lettering formed by putting a red background on the spine. No date on the title page. ". . . produced in 1957 by the Science Fiction Book Club . . ." on the copyright page.

d. (GRIFF NACH DER SONNE) [German], Abenteuer Im Weltenraum: 7, 1958, paper.

e. (IL DISCO DI FIÀMMA) [Italian], Urania: 193 (L150), 1958, paper.*
Translator: Laura Grimaldi.

f. _____, Ace: D-340 ($0.35), 1959, paper.*

g. (as WORLD OF CHANCE), Panther: 785 (2/6), 1959, paper.*
WORLD OF CHANCE version.

h. (LOTERIA SOLAR) [Spanish], Cenit: 4, 1960, paper.

i. (GRIFF NACH DER SONNE) [German], Terra Extra: 47, 1964, paper.

j. _____, Ace: G-718, ($0.50), 1968, paper.*

k. (LOTERIE SOLAIRE) [French], Galaxie Bis: 7, 1968, paper.

l. (TAIYO QUIZ) [Japanese], Hayakawa Shobo (Y270), 1968, paper. Translator: Obi Fusa.

m. (DE AARDE ALS HOOFDPRIJS) [Dutch], Born: SF 10 (Fl 3.15), 1969, paper. Translator: Frank Visser.

n. _____, Ace: 77410 ($0.50), 1970, paper.*

o. (IL DISCO DI FIAMMA) [Italian], Urania: 531 (L250), 1970, paper.* Translator: Laura Grimaldi.

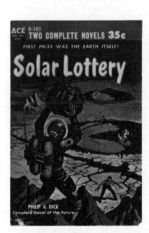  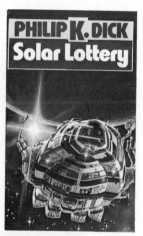

38.a.   38.u.   38.v.

p. (HAUPTGEWINN: DIE ERDE) [German], Goldmann: 0131, 1971, paper.* Translator: Hans-Ulrich Nichau. Reprinted 1975.

q. _____, Arrow: 905700 (30p), 1972, paper.*
SOLAR LOTTERY version?

r. (LOTERIE SOLAIRE) [French], J'ai Lu: 547, 1974, paper. Translator: Frank Straschitz. Reprinted 1978.

s. _____, Ace: 77411 ($1.25), 1975, paper.*

t. _____, Gregg Press, Boston ($9.50), 1976.*
Introduction by Thomas M Disch. Bound in dark green cloth with gold lettering on the spine. "First Printing, June 1976" on the copyright page. "1976" on the title page. Issued without dustjacket. Text is photo-reproduced from the 1955 Ace edition.

u. (IL DISCO DI FIAMMA) [Italian], Mondadori: Classici Fantascienza 15 (L1000), 1978, paper.* Translator: Laura Grimaldi.

v. _____, Arrow: 905700 (95p), 1979, paper.*
SOLAR LOTTERY version.

w. (   ) [Polish], Czytelnik, 1979 (?), paper (?).

39. EEN SWIBBEL VOOR DAG EN NACHT
Dutch collection.
Edited by Aart C. Prins.
Contents: Breakfast At Twilight; The Cosmic Poachers; Service Call; The Minority Report; The Commuter; The Days Of Perky Pat; Small Town.

39.a.   *40.a.*

a. _____, A W Bruna: 1295 (Fl 2.75), 1969, paper.*
Translator: CAG Van den Broek.

b. (as PHILIP K. DICK OMNIBUS), A W Bruna: SF 68, 1977, paper.
Combined with EEN HANDVOL DUISTERNIS (A HANDFUL OF DARKNESS).

40. THE THREE STIGMATA OF PALMER ELDRITCH
Nominated for 1965 Nebula for Best Novel.
Can-D allows the system's demoralized colonists to retreat into an ac-

ceptable fantasy analogue of Earth. Leo Bulero gets rich by supplying their needs. When Palmer Eldritch returns from the Prox system with a better drug, Leo is concerned and hostile. The new drug, Choo-Z, transports its users to universes of their own, which they can manipulate as they will. These universes all have a common god, however, and that god is Palmer Eldritch.

a. _____, Doubleday, Garden City ($4.95), 1965.*
Bound in light gray cloth with black lettering on the spine. "1965" on the title page. "First Edition" on the copyright page. Although this is a Doubleday book, and was published after Doubleday started to use date codes, there is no date code in this book. Also unusual for Doubleday, in this time frame, is the fact that the book is "perfect bound" (this is somewhat hidden by a headband). This first edition contains a page, not found in the book club edition, which lists current and forthcoming titles by Dick; some of these titles, such as THE FIRST LADY OF EARTH and IN THE MOLD OF YANCY, were apparently discarded before the books in question saw publication. The price printed on the dustjacket is $4.59 which, in all copies seen, has had a sticker placed over it stating "$4.95 D & CO. INC.".

40.n.

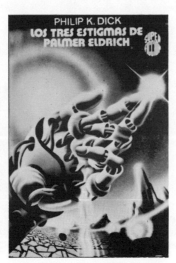

40.q.

40.o.

b. _____, Science Fiction Book Club, Garden City, 1965.*
Bound in gray paper boards with black lettering on the spine. Top edges stained blue. "1965" on title page. Perfect binding. No date code.

c. _____, Cape, London (21/-), 1966.*
Bound in light gray paper boards with gold lettering on the spine. No date on the title page. "First published in Great Britain 1966." on the copyright page.

d. _____, Macfadden: 60-240 ($0.60), 1966, paper.*

e. (LE DIEU VENU DU CENTAURE) [French], Opta: Anti-Mondes 12, 1969, paper (?).
Translator: Guy Abadia. Reprinted 1974.

f. (LE TRE STIMMATE DI PALMER ELDRITCH) [Italian], Libra Editrice, Bologna, 1970.*
Translator: Ugo Malaguti. Slan Libra 3. Reprinted 1976.
Bound in green paper boards with gold lettering on the front cover and spine.

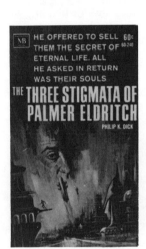

40.d.

40.p. – *frontis and title page.*

g. (LSD-ASTRONAUTEN) [German], Insel Verlag, Frankfurt (DM 14.50), 1971.*
Translator: Anneliese Strauss.
Bound in purple paper boards with silver lettering on the spine. Printed in purple ink.

h. _____, Macfadden: 75-399 ($0.75), 1971, paper.*

i. (DE DRIE STIGMATA VAN PALMER ELDRITCH) [Dutch], Born: SF 43, 1972, paper.

j. _____, Penguin: 3399 (30p), 1973, paper.*

k. _____, Manor: 12296 ($1.25), 1975, paper.*
Reprinted 1977.*

l. (LE DIEU VENU DU CENTAURE) [French], Marabout: 627, 1976, paper.
Published in Belgium.

m. _____, Bantam: 10586 ($1.75), 1977, paper.*

n. _____, Panther: 04584 (85p), 1978, paper.*

o. ( ) [Japanese], Hayakawa Shobo, Tokyo (Y1000), 1978.*
Bound in heavy, pebble-grained gray paper boards with dark blue lettering on the front cover and on the spine. Upon publication there was a purple banner (approximately 3 inches wide) wrapped around the dustjacket.

p. _____, Gregg Press, Boston ($14.95), 1979.*
Introduction by Paul Williams. Frontispiece by Hannah Shapero. Bound in dark green cloth with gold lettering on the spine. Title and author's name are on bright red background on the spine. Author's signature stamped in gold on the front cover. "First Printing, November 1979" on the copyright page. Issued without dustjacket. Text is photo-reproduced from the 1965 Doubleday edition.

q. (LOS TRES ESTIGMAS DE PALMER ELDRICH) [Spanish], Martinez Roca: SF 43, 1979, paper.*
Translator: Jordi Arbones.

r. ( ) [Greek], Exantas, 1979 (?), paper (?).

41. TIME OUT OF JOINT

Ragel Gumm believes himself to be a drone, living with his in-laws and supporting himself by anticipating patterns in a supposedly random newspaper contest. When Ragel accidentally breaks out of his carefully constructed reality, he discovers he is neither where, when nor whom he believes himself to be. His idle newspaper game is, in fact, the only thing preserving Earth's military dictatorship from destruction in the Lunar-Terran conflict.

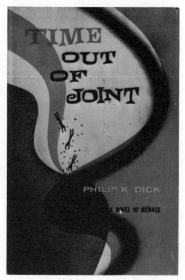

41.e.   41.m.   41.a.

a. _____, Lippincott, Philadelphia ($3.50), 1959.*
Bound in orange paper boards with black lettering on the spine and front cover. No date on the title page. "First Edition" on the copyright page.

b. (IL TEMPO SI E SPEZZATO) [Italian], I Romanzi del Corriere: 59 (L100), 1959, paper.*
Translator: Pinuccia Rebora.

c. _____, Science Fiction Book Club (British), London, 1961.

d. (ZEIT OHNE GRENZEN) [German], Zimmermann, 1962. Hardcover (?).

e. _____, Belmont: 92-618 ($0.50), 1965, paper.*

f. (L'UOMO DEI GIOCHI A PREMIO) [Italian], Urania: 491 (L250), 1968, paper.*
Translator: B della Frattina.

g. _____, Penguin: 002847 (25p, 5/-), 1969, paper.*

h. _____, Rapp & Whiting, London (28/-), 1970.*
Bound in black paper boards with silver lettering on the spine. Silver publisher's colophon on the front cover. "First published in Great Britain 1970" on the copyright page. No date on the title page.

i. (LE TEMPS DÉSARTICULE) [French], Calmann-Levy (29.00F), 1975, paper.*
Translator: Philippe R Hupp.

j. _____, Penguin: 002847 (50p), 1976, paper.*

k. _____, Belmont: BT51143 ($1.25), 1977, paper.

l. (LE TEMPS DÉSARTICULE) [French], Le Livre de Poche: 7021, 1978, paper.
Translator: Philippe R Hupp.

m. (ZEITLOSE ZEIT) [German], Goldmann: 23269 (DM 5.80), 1978, paper.*
Translator: Tony Westermayr.

n. (   ) [Japanese], Sanrio: 3-A (Y380), 1978, paper.*

o. _____, Gregg Press, Boston ($14.95), 1979.*
Introduction by Louis Stathis. Frontispiece by Hannah Shapero. Bound in dark green cloth with gold lettering on the spine. Title and author's name are on bright red background on the spine. Author's signature stamped in gold on the front cover. "First Printing, April 1979" on copyright page. Issued without dustjacket. Text is photo-reproduced from the 1959 Lippincott edition.

p. _____, Dell: 18860 ($2.25), 1979, paper.*

THE TRANSMIGRATION OF BISHOP TIMOTHY ARCHER
See BISHOP TIMOTHY ARCHER

THE TURNING WHEEL
See THE BOOK OF PHILIP K DICK

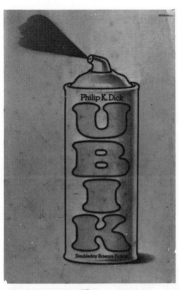

42.a.

42.d.

42. UBIK

Manuscript title "Death Of An Anti-Watcher".

Psis and anti-psis wage a commercial and political war for high stakes. Joe Chip, a psionic tester acting on an important mission for his partially deceased boss, Glen Runciter, discovers certain anomalies in the cosmos. People begin to fade, artifacts begin to turn stale and disappear, and a boy named Jory is transmitting his thoughts like powerful radio signals into Joe's mind. The only way Joe can stabilize the deteriorating world is to spray it with Ubik—compressed ubiquity.

a. _____, Doubleday, Garden City ($4.50), 1969.*
Bound in gray cloth with silver lettering on the spine. "1969" on the title page. "First Edition" on the copyright page. Date code "K10" (10th week of 1969) on page 202.

b. _____, Science Fiction Book Club, Garden City, 1969.*
Bound in gray paper boards with pink lettering on the spine. No date on the title page. Date code "28K" on lower left margin of unnumbered page 203.

c. _____, Dell: 9200 ($0.95), 1970, paper.*

d. _____, Rapp & Whiting, London (28/-), 1970.*
Bound in black paper boards with silver lettering on the spine. No date on the title page. "First published in Great Britain 1970" on the copyright page.

e. _____, [French], Laffont, Paris (16.70F), 1970, paper (?).
Translator: Alain Doremieux.

f. (UBIK, MIO SIGNORE) [Italian], Galassia: 175 (L400), 1972, paper.
Translator: G Montanari.

g. _____, Panther: 03716 (35p), 1973, paper.

h. _____, [Danish], Notabene, 1973, paper (?).
Translator: Jannick Storm.

i. _____, [Polish], Wydawnictwo Literackie, 1975, paper.*
Translator: Michal Ronikier. Illustrated by Jerzy Skarzynski.

j. _____, [French], J'ai Lu: 633, 1975, paper.*
Translator: Alain Doremieux.

k. _____, [Dutch], Meulenhoff: SF 94, 1975, paper.*
Translator: Paul Griffen.

42.c.

42.l.

42.m.

l. _____, [Spanish], Martinez Roca: SF 13, 1976, paper.*
Translator: Manuel Espin.

m. _____, Bantam: 10402 ($1.75), 1977, paper.*

n. _____, [German], Suhrkamp: 440, 1977, paper.*

o. _____, Panther: 03716 (75p), 1978, paper.*

p. _____, [Japanese], Hayakawa Shobo: SF 314 (Y360), 1978, paper.*
Translator: Hisashi Asakura.

q. _____, Gregg Press, Boston ($10.95), 1979.*
Introduction by Michael Bishop. Frontispiece by Hannah Shapero.
Bound in dark green cloth with gold lettering on the spine. Title and
author's name are on bright red background on the spine. Author's
signature stamped in gold on the front cover. "First Printing, April
1979" on the copyright page. Issued without dustjacket. Text is photo-
reproduced from the 1969 Doubleday edition.

43. THE UNTELEPORTED MAN

("The Unteleported Man", Fantastic, Dec 1964)

**Of the Sol system's two mega-corporations, one has already been gutted
and the other is still trying to stave off the German-run, fascistic United
Nations government. The government is using a mysterious one-way
teleportation system to populate a second Earth, but messages from this
colony have been proven to be fakes. Rachmael von Applebaum wants
to use the only remaining asset of his bankrupt corporation, an interstellar ship, to make the eighteen year physical journey to investigate
the fate of millions of colonists.**

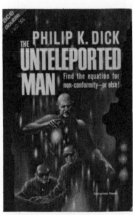
43.a.

43.c.

43.e.

a. _____, Ace: G-602 ($0.50), 1966, paper; with THE MIND MONSTERS (Howard L Cory).*

b. (UTOPIA ANDATA E RITORNO) [Italian], Galassia: 93 (L350), 1968, paper.
Translator: G Bonetti.

c. _____, Ace: 15697 ($0.95), 1972, paper; with DR. FUTURITY (Dick).*

d. _____, Methuen: 36550 (50p), 1976, paper.*

e. _____, Magnum: 04600 (80p), 1979, paper.*

f. (as LIES, INC.), Berkley.
This volume is to include the second half of the original manuscript which has never before been published. The title is tentative. Forthcoming.

44. VALIS

A coterie of religious seekers forms to explore the revelatory visions of one Horselover Fat; a semi-autobiographical analogue of PKD. The group's hermenutical research leads to a rock musician's estate where they confront the Messiah; a two-year-old named Sophia. She confirms their suspicions that an ancient, mechanical intelligence orbiting the Earth has been guiding their discoveries.

a. _____, Bantam: 14156 ($2.25), 1981, paper.*
"A Bantam Book / February 1981 // 0 9 8 7 6 5 4 3 2 1" on the copyright page. The first printing of 85,000 copies sold out by May.

b. (CIVA), [French], Denoël: 317, 1981, paper.*

c. _____, Bantam: 20594 ($2.50), 1981, paper.

45. THE VARIABLE MAN

Contents: The Variable Man; Second Variety; The Minority Report; Autofac; A World Of Talent.

a. _____, Ace: D-261 ($0.35), 1957, paper.*

b. (GUERRA CON CENTAURO) [Spanish], Cenit: 14, 1961, paper.

c. (KRIEG DER AUTOMATEN) [German], Terra: 322-323, 1964, paper.
Omits: A World Of Talent.

d. _____, Sphere: 29580 (6/-), 1969, paper.*

e. (L'HOMME VARIABLE) [French], Le Masque: 31, 1975, paper.
Omits: Autofac and A World Of Talent.

f. _____, Ace: 86050 ($1.50), 1976, paper.*

g. _____, Sphere: 2962 (75p),1977, paper.

h. _____, Sphere: 2962 (65p), 1978, paper.

i. (L'UOMO VARIABILE) [Italian], Fanucci: Futuro 45 (L3500), 1979, paper.*
   Translators: M Nati and T Tagliamonte.

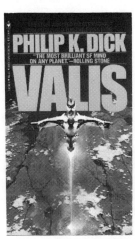

44.a.   45.a.   45.f.

46. VULCAN'S HAMMER

("Vulcan's Hammer", Future, No 29, 1956)

After the Atomic War, men turn over control of their society to Vulcan III, a computer. In the static civilization thus created, the Healers lead the lower strata of society in a revolution that threatens stability. There are also certain intimations that Vulcan III is not the impartial controller it once was, and that it will fight for its own survival.

a. _____, Ace: D-457 ($0.35), 1960, paper; with THE SKYNAPPERS (John Brunner).*

b. (VULCANO 3) [Italian], Urania: 320 (L200), 1963, paper.
   Translator: Beata della Frattina.

c. (VULKANS HAMMER) [German], Terra: 395, 1965, paper.

d. _____, Ace: 86608 ($0.75), 1972, paper.*

e. (DATORKRIGET) [Swedish], B Wahlstrom, 1972, paper (?).
   Translator: Tommy Schinkler.

f. (VULKAN 3) [German], Goldmann: 0170, 1973, paper.
   Translator: Tony Westermayr.

g. (LES MARTEAUX DE VULCAIN) [French], Le Masque: 28, 1974, paper.
   Translator: Monique Benatre.

h. _____, Arrow: 913300 (50p), 1976, paper.

i. (DE HAMER VAN DONAR) [Dutch], A W Bruna: SF 90, 1978, paper.*
Translator: Elly Schurink-Vooren.

j. (VULCANO 3) [Italian], Urania: 793, 1979, paper.
Translator: Beata della Frattina.

k. _____, Gregg Press, Boston ($11.95), 1979.*
Introduction by Fax Goodlife. Frontispiece by Hannah Shapero.
Bound in dark green cloth with gold lettering on the spine. Title and
author's name are on bright red background on the spine. Author's
signature stamped in gold on the front cover. "First Printing,
November 1979" on the copyright page. Issued without dustjacket.
Text is photo-reproduced from the 1960 Ace edition.

l. (A MAQUINA DE GOVERNAR) [Portuguese], Livros Do Brasil: 207, 19??,
paper.*
Published in Brazil.

46.a.   46.i.

47. WE CAN BUILD YOU
("A. Lincoln, Simulacrum", Amazing, sr2, Nov 1969)
**A fly-by-night musical instrument company produces a mechanical
replica of Edwin M. Stanton. The design of a neurotic girl and a deteri-
orated engineer, it fails to impress the shady entrepreneur who com-
missioned it. Next the factory builds a Lincoln simulacrum which
proves to be more in touch with reality than many of its builders.**

a. _____, DAW: 14 ($0.95), 1972, paper. Also numbered UQ1014.*
Reprinted.

b. _____, DAW: UY1164 ($1.25), 1975, paper.*

47.c.

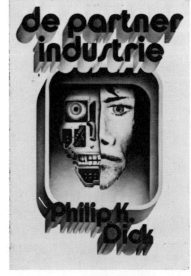

47.d.

47.a.

47.g.

47.f.

c. (LE BAL DES SCHIZOS) [French], Champ Libre: 8, 1975, paper.*
    Translators: Georges and Anned Dutter.

d. (DE PARTNER-INDUSTRIE) [Dutch], Born: SF 62, 1975, paper.*
    Translator: H J Oolbekkink.

e. (ABRAMO LINCOLN ANDROIDE) [Italian], Ciscato, Milan (L3800), 1976.
    Translators: G P Cossato and S Sandrelli. Gamma 16.

f. _____, Fontana: 614616 (70p), 1977, paper.*

g. (DIE REBELLISCHEN ROBOTER) [German], Goldmann: 0252, 1977, paper.*
Translator: Tony Westermayr.

h. (A COME ANDROIDE) [Italian], Ciscato, Milan (L3800), 1978.
Translators: G P Cossato and S Sandrelli.

48. THE WORLD JONES MADE
Manuscript title "Womb For Another".

48.*a.*   48.*h.*   48.*f.*

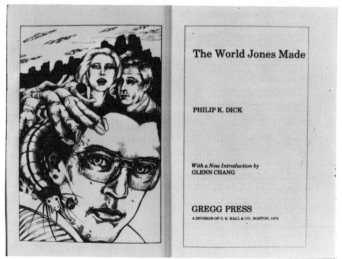

48.*o.* — *frontis and title page.*

Fed-gov is reconstructing the post-war world according to the precepts of relativism. Jones, a former carnival fortune-teller and preacher who can see a year into the future, says the alien drifters, origin unknown, are the greatest threat the world faces, a problem the Fed-gov refuses to deal with. Jones forms a fanatical organization to deal with the drifters and the Fed-gov.

a. _____, Ace: D-150 ($0.35), 1956, paper; with AGENT OF THE UNKNOWN (Margaret St. Clair).*

b. (GEHEIM PROJEKT VENUS) [German], Abenteuer Im Weltenraum: 8, 1958, paper.

c. (EL TIEMPO DOBLADE) [Spanish], Cenit: 3, 1963, paper.

d. (IL MONDO CHE JONES CREO) [Italian], Galassia: 50 (L300), 1965, paper. Translator: L Pollini.

e. (GEHEIM PROJEKT VENUS) [German], Terra Extra: 73, 1965, paper.

f. _____, Ace: F-429 ($0.40), 1967, paper.*

g. _____, Sidgwick & Jackson, London (18/-), 1968.*
Bound in dark red paper boards with gold lettering on spine. No date on the title page. "This edition published 1968 by // Sidgwick and Jackson Limited" on the copyright page.

h. _____, Panther: 02949 (25p, 5/-), 1970, paper.*

i. (DIE SELTSAME WELT DES MR. JONES) [German], Goldmann: 0126, 1971, paper.*
Translator: Tony Westermayr. Reprinted 1975.

j. (VLUCHT NAAR VENUS) [Dutch], Het Spectrum: Prisma 1472 (Fl 2.75), 1971, paper.*
Translator: Gerard Suurmeijer.

k. (LES CHAÎNES DE L'AVENIR) [French], La Masque: 41, 1975, paper.

l. _____, Ace: 90951 ($1.25), 1975, paper.*

m. _____, NEL: 98364 (60p), 1976, paper.*

n. (DE STERRENZWERVERS) [Dutch], Ridderhof, 1976, paper.

o. _____, Gregg Press, Boston ($12.95), 1979.*
Introduction by Glenn Chang. Frontispiece by Hannah Shapero. Bound in dark green cloth with gold lettering on the spine. Title and author's name are on bright red background on the spine. Author's signature stamped in gold on the front cover. "First Printing, November 1979" on the copyright page. Issued without dustjacket. Text is photo-reproduced from the 1956 Ace edition.

WORLD OF CHANCE
See SOLAR LOTTERY

49. THE ZAP GUN

("Project Plowshare", Worlds Of Tomorrow, sr2, Nov 1965)

Lars Powderdry is a mystic in a cold war world. He enters a trance and returns with new weapons designs for the Wes-Bloc powers. Some are plowshared, or disguised as innocuous items. Lars' Peep-East equivalent maintains the status quo with her own weapons, but the balance of tension cannot be preserved.

a. _____, Pyramid: R1569 ($0.50), 1967, paper.*

b. (MR. LARS, SOGNATORE D'ARMI) [Italian], Galassia: 109 (L350), 1970, paper.*
Translators: T Lanapopi and S Sandrelli.

c. (IN DE BAN VAN DE BOM) [Dutch], Born: SF 31, 1971, paper.*
Translator: H J Oolbekkink.

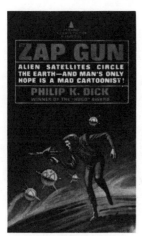  

49.*a.*   49.*e.*   49.*h.*

d. (DEDALUSMAN) [French], La Masque: 16, 1974, paper.
Translator: Raymond Albeck.

e. _____, Panther: 04112 (40p), 1975, paper.*
Reprinted 1976.

f. _____, Panther: 04112 (75p), 1978, paper.

g. _____, Dell: 19907 ($1.75), 1978, paper.*

h. (DAS LABYRINTH DER RATTEN) [German], Goldmann: 23300 (DM 5.80), 1979, paper.*
Translator: Tony Westermayr.

i. _____, Gregg Press, Boston ($12.95), 1979.*
Introduction by Charles Platt. Frontispiece by Hannah Shapero.
Bound in dark green cloth with gold lettering on the spine. Title and
author's name are on bright red background on the spine. Author's signature stamped in gold on the front cover. "First Printing, April 1979"
on the copyright page. Issued without dustjacket. Text is photo-
reproduced from the 1967 Pyramid edition.

Four additional foreign language editions were found for which the
corresponding American titles could not be identified.

Spanish

a. EL HOMBRE DEL PASSDO, Edhasa
The title means "The Man Of The Past" and it could be DR. FUTURITY
but this is not confirmed.

b. UN MUNDO DE TALENTO, Edhasa (50 ptas), 1967, paper.
The title means "A World Of Talent". It could be a separate collection
or all or part of THE VARIABLE MAN.

Turkish

a. UZAYDA SUIKAST, Okat Yayinevi (750 kr), 1971, paper (?).
Translator: Reha Pinar. 165 pages. The title means something like
"Conspiracy In Space."

b. YARATILAN DUNYA, Okat Yayinevi (750 kr), 1971, paper (?).
Translator: Reha Pinar. 159 pages. The title means something like
"The Created World."

THE MAGAZINE OF

Fantasy AND

Science Fiction

JULY

40¢

SPECIAL
SUMMER
ISSUE

CANTATA 140

a new short novel by

PHILIP K. DICK

ROBERT F. YOUNG

ROGER ZELAZNY

C. S. LEWIS

BRISKIN
for
PRESIDENT

"Cantata 140" — first magazine appearance. (See page 85, item 13.a.)

STORIES

1. **"A. Lincoln, Simulacrum"**

    Published as WE CAN BUILD YOU.

    A fly-by-night musical instrument company produces a mechanical replica of Edwin M. Stanton. The design of a neurotic girl and a deteriorated engineer, it fails to impress the shady entrepreneur who commissioned it. Next, the factory builds a Lincoln simulacrum that proves to be more in touch with reality than many of its builders.

    a. Amazing, sr2, Nov 1969, Jan 1970.*
    Illustrated by Mike Hinge.

1.a.   5.a.

2. **"The Above And Melting"**

    Verse.

    A short poem, about 12 lines as Dick remembers.

    a. A CHILD'S HAT, Ed by Ward J Gulyas, Published by the editor, 1966, paper.

3. **"Adjustment Team"** (7900 words)

    Ed Fletcher discovers a run in the fabric of events when his sector is de-energized and he is not inside it.

    a. Orbit Science Fiction, Sept-Oct 1954, No 4.*
    Illustrated by Faragasso.

    b. THE SANDS OF MARS AND OTHER STORIES (Australian), Jubilee Publications Pty Ltd., Sydney, undated (No 213, March 1958).*
    This is the third issue of the "Satellite Series", whose numbering started with No 211.

    c. THE BOOK OF PHILIP K. DICK, DAW: 44, 1973, paper.*

    d. (as "Squadra Riparazioni") [Italian], I DIFENSORI DELLA TERRA, Fanucci: Futuro 34, 1977, paper.*

4. **"The Alien Mind"** (850 words)
   Dick's shortest story.

   a. The Yuba City High Times, 20 Feb 1981.

   b. Fantasy & Science Fiction, Oct 1981.*
      Not illustrated.

5. **"All We Marsmen"** (87100 words)
   Published as MARTIAN TIME SLIP.

   The unions control Mars, the colonial world of speculation, and Arnie Kott the plumber is at the top of the heap. Arnie wants to use the time-warping abilities of Manfred, a schizophrenic child, to corner Martian real estate. Kott sets Jack Bolen the task of building a machine to communicate with Manfred. Instead, Manfred catches them up in a degenerating time-loop, fearing the vision of his own future. Only the telepathic Martians can communicate successfully with Manfred and aid him in escaping from a future that is gradually spreading back to obliterate the past.

   a. Worlds Of Tomorrow, sr3, Aug 1963, Oct 1963, Dec 1963.*
      Illustrated by Virgil Finlay (all three issues).

   b. (as "Nous Les Martiens") [French], Galaxie, New Series, sr3, Dec 1966, Jan 1967, Feb 1967, No 32, 33, 34.

6. **"The Android And The Human"**
   Non-Fiction.
   Speech delivered at the Vancouver SF Convention at the University of British Columbia, March 1972.

   PKD discusses the concept of convergence in mechanical and human awareness. He states the quality of unpredictability will always distinguish the human mind. In a look at the totalitarian state, he welcomes the prospect of civil disobedience. A strong anti-drug statement is also made here.

   a. SF Commentary 31, Dec 1972.*

   b. Vector, No 64, March-April 1973.

   c. PHILIP K DICK: ELECTRIC SHEPHERD, Ed by Bruce Gillespie, Norstrilia Press, 1975, paper.*

   d. (as "Androiden Und Menschen") [German], Science Fiction Times, Special Issue No 1: PHILIP K DICK—MATERIALIEN, 1976.*

   e. (as "L'Homme Et L'Androide") [French], INCONSCIENCE FICTION, Ed by Boris Eizkman, Kesselring, 1979, paper.*

7. **"Anthony Boucher"**
   Non-Fiction.

   a. Fantasy & Science Fiction, Aug 1968.*

8. **"Autofac"** (9000 words)

   The factories had been designed to supply human needs in a war-torn world. With the war over, the factories still supply everything automatically: a kind of utopia. Men, however, wish to resume control of their own means of production—but the factories possess a mechanical vitality and some very human characteristics.

   "Tom Disch said of this story that it was one of the earliest ecology warnings in sf. What I had in mind in writing it, however, was the thought that if factories became fully automated, they might begin to show the instinct for survival which organic living entities have . . . and perhaps develop similar solutions."—PKD

   a. Galaxy, Nov 1955.*
      Illustrated by Ed Emshwiller.

   b. (as "Le Regne Des Robots") [French], Galaxie, Old Series, Aug 1956, No 33.

   c. THE VARIABLE MAN, Ace: D-261, 1957, paper.*

   d. [Italian], Galaxy, No 8, 1959.

   e. THE RUINS OF EARTH, Ed by Thomas M Disch, Putnam, New York ($6.95), 1971.*

   f. BEYOND CONTROL, Ed by Robert Silverberg, Thomas Nelson, New York, ($5.95), 1972.*

   g. (as "Autofab") [Dutch], ALFA EEN, Meulenhoff: SF 66, 1973, paper.*

   h. (as "Le Regne Des Robots") [French], Marginal, Sept-Oct 1974, No 5.

   i. SCIENCE FACT/FICTION, Ed by Farrell, Gage, Pfordresher and Rodriques, Scott Foresman and Company ($4.95), 1974, paper.

   j. THE BEST OF PHILIP K. DICK, Ballantine: 25359, 1977, paper.*

   k. [Italian], L'UOMO VARIABILE, Fanucci: Futuro 45, 1979, paper.*

9. **"Beyond Lies The Wub"** (2650 words)

   Author's first published story.

   The captain wants to butcher and eat the wub because of a food shortage. The wub, who is intelligent, telepathic and affable, agrees.

   "My first published story, in the most lurid of all pulp magazines on the stands at the time, Planet Stories. As I carried four copies into the record store where I worked, a custumer gazed at me and them, with dismay, and said, 'Phil, you read **that** *kind of stuff?' I had to admit I not only read it, I wrote it."*—PKD

   a. Planet Stories, July 1952.*

   b. (as "Ou Se Niche Le Wub") [French], Univers, No 11, 1952 (?).

   c. THE PRESERVING MACHINE, Ace: 67800, 1969, paper.*

   d. ALPHA 3, Ed by Robert Silverberg, Ballantine: 02883 ($1.25), 1972, paper.*

e. (as "Het Goffermaal") [Dutch], DE ONMOGELIJKE PLANEET, A W Bruna: SF 40, 1976, paper.*

f. (as "Ora Tocca Al Wub") [Italian], LE VOCI DI DOPO, Fanucci: Futuro 26, 1976, paper.*

g. THE BEST OF PHILIP K. DICK, Ballantine: 25359, 1977, paper.*

h. (as "Mas Alla Yace El Web") [Spanish], LA MAQUINA PRESERVADORA, Edhasa: 23, 1978, paper.*

9.a. — interior.   13.a.

10. "Beyond The Door" (2700 words)

An intelligent cuckoo-clock serves as the pivot for a love and hate triangle.

a. Fantastic Universe, Jan 1954.*

11. "Breakfast At Twilight" (6200 words)

The McLean's house is accidentally sucked forward through time to the middle of a nuclear war.

"There you are in your home, and the soldiers smash down the door and tell you you're in the middle of World War III. Something's gone wrong with time. I like to fiddle with the idea of basic categories of reality, such as space and time, breaking down. It's my love of chaos, I suppose."—PKD

    a. Amazing, July 1954.*

    b. Amazing (British), Third Series, Vol 1 No 6, undated (Oct 1954).

    c. Fantastic, Nov 1966.*

    d. (as "Ontbijt In De Schemering") [Dutch], EEN SWIBBEL VOOR DAG EN NACHT, A W Bruna: 1295, 1969, paper.*

    e. THE BOOK OF PHILIP K. DICK, DAW: 44, 1973, paper.*

    f. THE BEST OF PHILIP K. DICK, Ballantine: 25359, 1977, paper.*

    g. (as "Colazione Al Crepuscolo") [Italian], I DIFENSORI DELLA TERRA, Fanucci: Futuro 34, 1977, paper.*

12. "The Builder" (4500 words)

In a decadent world suspiciously like our own, Elwood works under some unknown inspiration to build a boat.

    a. Amazing, Dec 1953-Jan 1954.*
       Illustration by Ed Emshwiller.

    b. Amazing (British), Third Series, Vol 1 No 3, undated (April 1954).

    c. A HANDFUL OF DARKNESS, Rich & Cowan, London, 1955.*

    d. Amazing, June 1967.*

    e. (as "De Doe-Het-Zelver") [Dutch], EEN HANDVOL DUISTERNIS, A W Bruna: 1100, 1968, paper.*

    f. (as "Le Constructeur") [French], Fiction, Aug 1972, No 224.*

13. "Cantata 140" (22000 words)

First half of THE CRACK IN SPACE.

Frozen sleep seems like a humane way to end unemployment and over-population pressures: Send the excess citizens to the future. Government warehouses are filled with bibs and a political fight erupts over whether or not to dispose of them through a space-warp. Then an unknown agency begins to help the sleepers to awake.

    a. Fantasy & Science Fiction, July 1964.*
       Cover art for "Cantata 140" by Ed Emshwiller. Story not illustrated.

    b. [French], Fiction, Feb 169, No 182.

14. "Captive Market" (6600 words)

Old Mrs Berthelsen does some very profitable business by driving her truck into an alternate continuum. It continues to be profitable because she can pick any time track she wishes.

    a. If, April 1955.*
       Illustrated by Kelly Freas.

b. THE FIRST WORLD OF IF, Ed by James L Quinn and Eve Wulf, Quin ($0.50), 1957, paper.*
Magazine format.

c. THE PRESERVING MACHINE, Ace: 67800, 1969, paper.*

d. TOMORROW, INC., Ed by Martin Harry Greenberg and Joseph D Olander, Taplinger, New York ($9.95), 1976.

e. (as "Monopolie") [Dutch], DE ONMOGELIJKE PLANEET, A W Bruna: SF 40, 1976, paper.*

f. (as "Commercio Temporale") [Italian], LE VOCI DI DOPO, Fanucci: Futuro 26, 1976, paper.*

g. (as "El Cliente Perfecto") [Spanish], EN LA TIERRA SOMBRIA, Edhasa: 26, 1978, paper.*

h. (as "Clientele Captive") [French], LES DÉLIRES DIVERGENTS DE PHILIP K. DICK, Ed by Alain Doremieux, Casterman, Paris, 1979.*

15. "Chains Of Air, Web Of Aether"

Became part of THE DIVINE INVASION.
Rybus Rommey's need for solace in the course of a serious illness cuts through Leo McVane's immaculate barriers of isolation.

a. STELLAR #5, Ed by Judy-Lynn del Rey, Ballantine: 28065 ($1.95), 1980, paper.*

16. "The Chromium Fence" (5750 words)

The world is galvanized into two distinct factions over the Horney Amendment; a measure to control hygienics and personal cleanliness. Fist-fights, threats and coercion are the order of the day, with death in store for the losing side.

a. Imagination, July 1955.*
Illustrated by W E Terry (?).

17. "Colony" (6400 words)

An exploration crew finds one dangerous life-form on an otherwise idyllic world. The organism can imitate any organic object, no matter the size.

*"The ultimate in paranoia is not when everyone is against you but when every**thing** is against you. Instead of 'My boss is plotting against me,' it would be 'My boss's phone is plotting against me.' Objects sometimes seem to possess a will of their own anyhow, to the normal mind; they don't do what they're supposed to do, they get in the way, they show an unnatural resistance to change. In this story I tried to figure out a situation which would rationally explain the dire plotting of objects against humans, without reference to any deranged state on the part of the humans. I guess you'd have to go to another planet. The ending on this story is the ultimate victory of a plotting object over innocent people."—PKD*

a. Galaxy, June 1953.*
   Illustrated by Ed Emshwiller.

b. Galaxy (British), Vol 3 No 8, Oct 1953.*

c. (as "Kolonie") [German], Galaxis, No 7, undated, 1954 (?).*

d. (as "Defense Passive") [French], Galaxie, Old Series, Sept 1954, No 10.

e. A HANDFUL OF DARKNESS, Rich & Cowan, London, 1955.*

f. (as "Le Presenze Invisibli") [Italian], Urania No 72, 1955.
   Translator: Tom Arno.

g. (as "De Kolonie") [Dutch], EEN HANDVOL DUISTERNIS, A W Bruna:
   1100, 1968, paper.*

h. (as "Colonie") [French], Marginal, Nov-Dec 1973, No 1.

i. SPACE OPERA, Ed by Brian W Aldiss, Orbit: 058 (50p), 1974, paper.*

j. (as "De Kolonie") [Dutch], DE ONMOGELIJKE PLANEET, A W Bruna: SF
   40, 1976, paper.*

k. THE BEST OF PHILIP K. DICK, Ballantine: 25359, 1977, paper.*

18. "The Commuter" (4800 words)
A commuter, searching for his home, crosses over to an alternate continuum and upsets the balance of equilibrium between realities.

a. Amazing, Aug-Sept 1953.*

b. Amazing (British), Third Series, Vol 1 No 1, undated (Dec 1953).

c. Amazing, Dec 1966.*

d. (as "Il Sobborgo Dimenticato") [Italian], Urania No 466, 1967.
   Translator: B della Frattina.

e. (as "De Forens") [Dutch], EEN SWIBBEL VOOR DAG EN NACHT, A W
   Bruna: 1295, 1969, paper.*

f. THE BOOK OF PHILIP K. DICK, DAW: 44, 1973, paper.*

g. BEYOND TOMORROW, Ed by Lee Harding, Wren, South Melbourne,
   1976.

h. (as "Il Pendolare") [Italian], I DIFENSORI DELLA TERRA, Fanucci:
   Futuro 34, 1977, paper.*

i. (as "Le Banlieusard") [French], LE LIVRE D'OR DE LA SCIENCE-FICTION:
   PHILIP K. DICK, Ed by Marcel Thaon, Presses Pocket: 5051, 1979,
   paper.*

19. "The Cookie Lady" (3000 words)
Psychic vampires do not always appear in the guise of European nobility. This one is just a tiny old lady who means no harm.

a. Fantasy Fiction, June 1953.*

b. A HANDFUL OF DARKNESS, Rich & Cowan, London, 1955.*

c. MORE MACABRE, Ed by Donald A Wollheim, Ace: D-508, ($0.35), 1961, paper.*

d. (as "Koekjes") [Dutch], EEN HANDVOL DUISTERNIS, A W Bruna: 1100, 1968, paper.*

e. (as "La Dame Aux Biscuits") [French], Fiction, Jan 1970, No 193.

20. "The Cosmic Poachers" (3600 words)

The Sirius system has been closed to all but Terran vessels. When the insectile Adharans appear and scurry about on each Sirian planet, the Terran Patrol assumes they are taking, not giving.

a. Imagination, July 1953.*
Illustrated by W E Terry.

b. ALIEN WORLDS, Ed by Roger Elwood, Paperback: 52-320 ($0.50), 1964, paper.*

c. (as "Kapers In De Kosmos") [Dutch], EEN SWIBBEL VOOR DAG EN NACHT, A W Bruna: 1295, 1969, paper.*

21. "The Crack In Space"

First published as THE CRACK IN SPACE.

Frozen sleep seems like a humane way to end unemployment and over-population pressures; send the excess citizens to the future. The government warehouses are filled with bibs when a political fight erupts over whether to dispose of them through a space-warp. Then some outside agency helps the sleepers to awake.

a. A PHILIP K. DICK OMNIBUS, Sidgwick & Jackson, London, 1970.*

b. SCIENCE FICTION SPECIAL 7, Anonymous, Sidgwick & Jackson, London, 1973 (?).

22. "The Crawlers" (2800 words)

Radiation from Oak Ridge spawns mutant worm-like children. Those not murdered by their own fathers are segregated on an island. The mutants have their own destiny and their own devices, but they are not a separate species.

a. Imagination, July, 1954.*
Illustrated by W E Terry.

b. (as "Vittima Designata") [Italian], Urania No 59, 1954.
Translator: Tom Arno.

c. THE PRESERVING MACHINE, Ace: 67800, 1969, paper.*

d. YOU AND SCIENCE FICTION, Ed by Bernard Hollister, National Textbook Company, 1976, paper.*

e. (as "De Kruipers") [Dutch], DE ONMOGELIJKE PLANEET, A W Bruna: SF 40, 1976, paper.*

f. (as "Quelli Che Strisciano") [Italian], LE VOCI DI DOPO, Fanucci: Futuro 26, 1976, paper.*

g. (as "Los Reptiles") [Spanish], EN LA TIERRA SOMBRIA, Edhasa: 26, 1978, paper.*

h. (as "Los Rampants") [French], LES DÉLIRES DIVERGENTS DE PHILIP K. DICK, Ed by Alain Doremieux, Casterman, Paris, 1979.*

23. **"The Crystal Crypt"** (7750 words)
War was imminent. Terran agents had been spotted near the Martian capital. Suddenly the city was no more—vanished . . . and the last Terran ship was ready to leave Mars.

a. Planet Stories, Jan 1954.*
Illustrated by Kelly Freas.

24. **"The Days Of Perky Pat"** (7000 words)
Manuscript title "In The Days Of Perky Pat".

Post-war colonists survive on Earth only through Martian welfare. The colonists try to re-discover their lost culture and make life bearable by directed play with models and dolls representing their lost world.
"It was the Barbie-doll craze which induced this story, needless to say. Barbie always seemed unnecessarily real to me. Years later I had a girl friend whose ambition was to be a Barbie doll. I hope she made it."—PKD

a. Amazing, Dec 1963.*
Illustrated by Adkins.

b. The Most Thrilling Science Fiction Ever Told, Summer 1968, No 9.*

c. (as "De Tijd Van Hippe Hetty") [Dutch], EEN SWIBBEL VOOR DAG EN NACHT, A W Bruna: 1295, 1969, paper.*

d. THE BEST OF PHILIP K. DICK, Ballantine: 25359, 1977, paper.*

e. (as "Au Temps De Poupee Pat") [French], LE LIVRE D'OR DE LA SCIENCE-FICTION: PHILIP K. DICK, Ed by Marcel Thaon, Presses Pocket: 5051, 1979, paper.*

25. **"The Defenders"** (8600 words)
The underground cities of THE PENULTIMATE TRUTH are locked into a delusion of continuing Atomic war. Their mechanical soldiers are the first to recognize its futility.

a. Galaxy, Jan 1953.*
Cover art and story illustration for "The Defenders" by Ed Emshwiller.

b. Galaxy (British), Vol 3 No 5, June 1953.

   c. (as "Die Verteidiger") [German], Galaxis, No 5, undated, 1954 (?).*

   d. (as "Les Defenseurs") [French], Galaxie, New Series, Sept 1964, No 5.

   e. INVASION OF THE ROBOTS, Ed by Roger Elwood, Paperback: 52-519 ($0.50), 1965, paper.*

   f. (as "La Guerra Continua") [Italian], LA FANTAGUERRA, De Carlo, Milan (L6000), 1967.
     Translator: C Carrega.

   g. THE BOOK OF PHILIP K. DICK, DAW: 44, 1973, paper.*

   h. (as "I Difensori Della Terra") [Italian], I DIFENSORI DELLA TERRA, Fanucci: Futuro 34, 1977, paper.*

24.a.

25.a.

26. "Dr. Bloodmoney, Or How We Got Along After The Bomb"

First published as DR. BLOODMONEY, OR HOW WE GOT ALONG AFTER THE BOMB.

A post-nuclear war society struggles to reconstruct itself in an isolated setting. Kept in contact with the outside world by an orbiting disc-jockey, the group's members include Bill, an encysted telepathic twin; Bruno Bluthgeld, the weapons expert responsible for the war; and Hoppy Harrington, a phocomelus who makes a frightening power play for domination of the colony.

   a. (as "Cronache Del Dopobomba") [Italian], MILLEMONDINVERNO 1975: TRE ROMANZI COMPLETI DI PHILIP K. DICK, Mondadori: Supplemento A Urania 684, 1975, paper.*

27. "Dr. Futurity"

First published as DR. FUTURITY.

A time machine pulls a twenty-first century doctor four hundred years into the future. The science of medicine is then unknown because of a eugenics and voluntary euthanasia scheme. Parsons, the doctor, becomes involved in a complex time-hopping plot to change the course of the past by assassinating Sir Francis Drake.

a. A PHILIP K. DICK OMNIBUS, Sidgwick & Jackson, London, 1970.*

b. SCIENCE FICTION SPECIAL 7, Anonymous, Sidgwick & Jackson, London, 1973 (?).

28. "Drugs, Hallucinations, And The Quest For Reality"

Non-Fiction.

Dick discusses mental illnesses, especially those that include delusional systems and psychotic split.

a. Lighthouse, No 11, Nov 1964.

29. "The Electric Ant"

After an accident, Poole discovers he is not a man, but an organic robot. In his chest, a roll of punched tape supplies his reality, and he cannot resist altering the tape.

"Again the theme: How much of what we call 'reality' is actually out there or rather within our own head? The ending of this story has always frightened me . . . the image of the rushing wind, the sound of emptiness. As if the character hears the final fate of the world itself."—PKD

a. Fantasy & Science Fiction, Oct 1969.*
Not Illustrated.

b. (as "Formiche Elettriche") [Italian], Urania No 534, 1969 (?).
Translator: A Campana.

c. BEST SF: 1969, Ed by Harry Harrison and Brian W Aldiss, Putnam, New York ($5.95), 1970.*

d. (as "La Fourni Electronique") [French], Fiction, June 1970, No 198.

e. WINDOWS INTO TOMORROW, Ed by Robert Silverberg, Hawthorn, New York ($6.95), 1974.*

f. (as "De Elektrische Mier") [Dutch], ALFA DRIE, Ed by Warner Flamen, Meulenhoff: SF 96, 1975, paper.

g. THE BEST OF PHILIP K. DICK, Ballantine: 25359, 1977, paper.*

h. DECADE THE 1960s, Ed by Brian W Aldiss and Harry Harrison, Macmillan, London (£3.95), 1977.

i. THE ANDROIDS ARE COMING, Ed by Robert Silverberg, Elsevier/Nelson, New York ($7.95), 1979.*

30. "The Evolution Of A Vital Love"
Non-Fiction.

    a. Supplement to Mike Bailey's Personalzine, Numbers 20 and 21, May 1975.*
       This set of fanzines had no series title, but they were numbered. Each number had its own individual title. No 20 was titled The Long Goodbye. No 21 is believed to have been titled The Long Hello (?).

    b. (as "Die Entwicklung Einer Liebe") [German], Science Fiction Times, Special Issue No 1: PHILIP K. DICK—MATERIALIEN, 1976.*
       Translator: Uwe Anton.

31. "Exhibit Piece" (5400 words)
George Miller is the curator of the Twentieth Century history exhibit and is totally absorbed by his work. One day he steps inside his display and into a world two hundred years old; a world as superficially real as his own.

    a. If, Aug 1954.*
       Illustrated by Paul Orban.

    b. If (British), Vol 1 No 13, undated (Nov 1954).

    c. (as "Reconstitution Historique") [French], APRÈS DEMAIN LA TERRE, Ed by Alain Doremieux, Casterman, 1954 (?), paper.

    d. A HANDFUL OF DARKNESS, Rich & Cowan, London, 1955.*

32. "The Exit Door Leads In"

32.a.

Bob Bibleman is manipulated by his totalitarian government through the agency of an insolently programmed robot. He is sent to college, where he is tested for loyalty, learning that even a fascist government wants to be loved for the right reasons.

a. Rolling Stone College Papers, Fall 1979, No 1.*

b. (as   ) [French], Opzone, March 1980, No 7.

c. THE BEST SCIENCE FICTION OF THE YEAR #9, Ed by Terry Carr, Ballantine: 28601 ($2.50), 1980, paper.*

33. "Expendable" (2350 words)

Before Man colonized the Earth, insects were in control. Man has some allies he is unaware of when the insects start the war to regain their own.

"I loved to write short fantasy stories in my early days—for Anthony Boucher—of which this is my favorite. I got the idea when a fly buzzed by my head one day and I imagined (paranoia indeed!) that it was laughing at me."—PKD

a. Fantasy & Science Fiction, July 1953.*
   Not illustrated.

b. Fantasy & Science Fiction (British), Vol 1 No 4, Jan 1954.*

c. (as "Le Sacrifie") [French], Fiction, March 1954, No 4.

d. A HANDFUL OF DARKNESS, Rich & Cowan, London, 1955.*

e. Fantasy & Science Fiction (Australian), No 4, undated (Aug 1955).

f. SCIENCE FICTION SHOWCASE, Ed by Mary Kornbluth, Doubleday, Garden City ($3.95), 1959.

g. (as "Slachtoffer") [Dutch], EEN HANDVOL DUISTERNIS, A W Bruna: 1100, 1968, paper.*

h. THE BEST OF PHILIP K. DICK, Ballantine: 25359, 1977, paper.*

34. "Explorers We" (4000 words)

When the astronauts return from Mars, everyone flees from them. Finally, they are burned down by the F.B.I. This is the twenty-first time the same creatures have returned.

a. Fantasy & Science Fiction, Jan 1959.*
   Not illustrated.

b. (as "Le Retour Des Explorateurs") [French], Fiction, April 1965, No 137.

35. "The Eyes Have It" (1300 words)

Aliens are discovered in the literal interpretation of a mss. found on a bus.

a. Science Fiction Stories, No 1, 1953.*
   Not illustrated.

36. **"Fair Game"** (5000 words)

A physicist is singled out by god-like beings for a very prosaic purpose.

    a. If, Sept 1959.*
       Not illustrated.

37. **"Faith Of Our Fathers"**

Nominated for 1967 Hugo for Best Novelette.

The future is totalitarian: dominated utterly by the Chairman, and as venal and terrifying as our worst nightmares. The citizens are maintained in a state of hallucinogenic delusion. There are fears the Chairman is non-Terran, and Tung Chien discovers it may be another order of creature entirely; one against whom there is no defense.

"The title is that of an old hymn. I think, with this story, I managed to offend everybody, which seemed at the time to be a good idea, but which I've regretted since. Communism, drugs, sex, God — I put it all together, and it's been my impression since that when the roof fell in on me years later, this story was in some eerie way involved." — PKD

    a. DANGEROUS VISIONS, Ed by Harlan Ellison, Doubleday, Garden City ($6.95), 1967.*
       Illustrated by Leo & Diane Dillon.
       The Signet editions (1975 on) have an expanded afterword by Dick in which he rebuts a remark attributed to Harlan Ellison.

    b. (as "La Foi De Nos Peres") [French], Fiction, Aug 1969, No 188.

    c. ALPHA 2, Ed by Robert Silverberg, Ballantine: 02419 ($0.95), 1971, paper.*

    d. MODERN SCIENCE FICTION, Ed by Norman Spinrad, Anchor: A-978 ($3.50), 1974, paper.*

    e. THE BEST OF PHILIP K. DICK, Ballantine: 25359, 1977, paper.*

38. **"The Father-Thing"** (5100 words)

Charles's father walks into the garage — and an imitation walks out. With some friends' help, Charles destroys the bug that controls the imitation and also the pulpy pods that are growing his and his mother's replacements. (Published a year before Jack Finney's [INVASION OF] THE BODY SNATCHERS.)

"I always had the impression, when I was very small, that my father was two people, one good, one bad. The good father goes away and the bad father replaces him. I guess many kids have this feeling. What if it were so? This story is another instance of a normal feeling, which is in fact incorrect, somehow becoming correct . . . with the added misery that one cannot communicate it to others. Fortunately, there are other kids to tell it to. Kids understand: they are wiser than adults — hmmm, I almost said, 'Wiser than humans.' " — PKD

    a. Fantasy & Science Fiction, Dec 1954.*
       Not illustrated.

b. (as "Le Père Truque") [French], Fiction, April 1956, No 29.
Cover art for "The Father Thing" by Philippe Curval.
The French translations added a sentence at the end of the story: ". . . *Hundreds of kilometers from here another beast similar to the first one was emerging from its underground tunnel and was going to burrow itself inside a refuse dump." (. . . À dès centaines de kilomètres de là, une autre bête semblable à la premiere sortait de son souterrain et allait se terrer au creux d'un dépotoir.).*

c. (as "Le Père Truque") [French], LES UNIVERS DE LA SF, Ed by Hubert Juin, Club des Libraires de France, 1957.

d. A TREASURY OF GREAT SCIENCE FICTION — Volume 1, Ed by Anthony Boucher, Doubleday, Garden City, 1959.*

e. (as "Le Père Truque") [French], LES VINGT MEILLEURS RECITS DE SF, Ed by Hubert Juin, Marabout, 1964, paper.

f. (as "Le Père Truque") [French], LES CHEFS-D'OEUVRE DE L'ÉPOUVANTE, Ed by Jacques Sternberg, et al, Ed Planete, 1965.

g. THE UNHUMANS, Ed by Marvin Allen Kapp, Popular Library: SP-405 ($0.50), 1965, paper.*

h. TOMORROW'S CHILDREN, Ed by Isaac Asimov, Doubleday, Garden City ($4.95), 1966.*

i. THEMES IN SCIENCE FICTION, Ed by Leo P Kelley, Webster/McGraw-Hill ($2.45), 1972, paper.*

j. SOCIAL PROBLEMS THROUGH SCIENCE FICTION, Ed by Martin H Greenberg, John W Milstead, Joseph D Olander and Patricia S Warrick, St Martin's, New York, 1975.

k. THE BEST OF PHILIP K. DICK, Ballantine: 25359, 1977, paper.*

l. SCIENCE FICTION: CONTEMPORARY MYTHOLOGY, Ed by Patricia Warrick, Martin Harry Greenberg and Joseph Olander, Harper & Row, 1978, paper.*

39. "Foster, You're Dead"

Consumerism and advertising have adapted themselves to the cold war. Everyone is told to study survival, buy a shelter and not be anti-protection. Young Mike Foster is never as happy as when he is underground in his parents' bomb-shelter.

"One day I saw a newspaper headline reporting that the President suggested that if Americans had to **buy** *their bomb shelters, rather than being provided with them by the government, they'd take better care of them, an idea which made me furious. Logically, each of us should own a submarine, a jet fighter, and so forth. Here I just wanted to show how cruel the authorities can be when it comes to human life, how they can think in terms of dollars, not people."* — PKD

a. STAR SCIENCE FICTION STORIES NO 3, Ed by Frederick Pohl, Ballantine, New York ($2.00), 1955.*
Bound in green cloth with blue lettering on the spine. No date on title page. No indication of printing on copyright page.
Also published as Ballantine: 96 ($0.35), 1955, paper.*

b. (as   ) [Russian], Ogonek, April 1958.
The author's complimentary copy was destroyed by the U.S. Post Office as Communist propaganda.

c. (as "Foster, Esti Mort!") [Rumanian], Povestiri Stiintifico-Fantastice, June 1958, No 82.
Apparently translated from the Russian.

d. (as "Foster, Je Bent Dood") [Dutch], SCIENCE FICTION-VERHALEN, Het Spectrum: Prisma 633, 1961, paper.

e. (as "Foster, Vous Êtes Mort!"), [French], HISTOIRES DE FIN DU MONDE, Ed by Jacques Goimard, Le Livre de Poche, 1974, paper.

f. THE BEST OF PHILIP K. DICK, Ballantine: 25359, 1977, paper.*

40. "Frozen Journey"

Due to shipboard cryonics malfunctions, Victor Kemmings faces ten years trapped in a super-samadhi tank. Fighting brain deterioration, the computer takes Victor back into childhood and marriage, then desperately forward, through painful fantasy to, alas, the end of the journey.

a. Playboy, Dec 1980.*

b. THE BEST SCIENCE FICTION OF THE YEAR #10, Ed by Terry Carr, Pocket Books: 42262 ($3.50), 1981, paper.*
A Timescape Book.

41. "A Game Of Unchance" (8700 words)

An outsystem carnival unloads some hostile micro-robots on the Martian colonists in a psycho-kinetically rigged game of skill.

"A carnival is feral; another carnival shows up and is pitted against the first one; and the antithetical interaction is preplanned in such a way that the first carnival wins. It's as if the two opposing forces that underlie all change in the universe are rigged; in favor of thanatos, the dark force, yin or strife, which is to say, the force of destruction."—PKD

a. Amazing, July 1964.*
Illustrated by Schelling.

b. SF Greats, Fall 1970, No 19.

c. (as "Jeu De Malchance") [French], LE LIVRE D'OR DE LA SCIENCE-FICTION: PHILIP K. DICK, Ed by Marcel Thaon, Presses Pocket: 5051, 1979, paper.*

d. THE GOLDEN MAN, Ed by Mark Hurst, Berkley: 04288, 1980, paper.*

42. "A Glass Of Darkness" (4100 words)

Opening slightly changed when published as THE COSMIC PUPPETS.

Ted Barton returns to the isolated town of his youth. He finds it subtly different. Places and people have been added, and some have been taken away. A few of the inhabitants have strange god-like powers, and the intelligence controlling the town will not let anyone escape.

a. Satellite Science Fiction, Dec 1956.*
    Cover art for "A Glass Of Darkness" by Kelly Freas. Story illustrated by Arnold Arlow.

b. (as "La Citta Sostituita") [Italian], MILLEMONDINVERNO 1975: TRE ROMANZI COMPLETI DI PHILIP K. DICK, Mondadori: Supplemento A Urania 684, 1975, paper.*

43. "The Golden Man" (11600 words)

The Golden Man is a product of a post-atomic-war world. A proscribed mutant, his clairvoyant powers may make him more fit to survive than the rest of humanity.

"Here I am saying that mutants are dangerous to us ordinaries, a view which John W. Campbell, Jr. deplored. We were supposed to view them as our leaders. But I always felt uneasy as to how they would view us. I mean, maybe they wouldn't **want** *to lead us. Maybe from their superevolved lofty level we wouldn't seem worth leading. Anyhow, even if they agreed to lead us, I felt uneasy as to where we would wind up going. It might have something to do with buildings marked SHOWERS but which really weren't."*
—PKD

43.a. — interior.

a. If, April 1954.*
    Illustrated by Kelly Freas.

b. If (British), Vol 1 No 9, undated (July 1954).

c. BEYOND THE BARRIERS OF SPACE AND TIME, Ed by Judith Merril, Random House, New York ($2.95), 1954.*

d. STRANGE GIFTS, Ed by Robert Silverberg, Thomas Nelson, New York ($6.95), 1975.

e. EVIL EARTHS, Ed by Brian W Aldiss, Weidenfeld & Nicholson, London (£4.25), 1975.*

f. THE GOLDEN MAN, Ed by Mark Hurst, Berkley: 04288, 1980, paper.*

44. "The Great C" (4900 words)

Parts of this story were adapted for DEUS IRAE.

Each year, a youth from the tribe must ask the computer three questions. If the computer can answer, the youth's body goes to feed the circuits. This year's first question is: "Where does the rain come from?"

a. Cosmos Science Fiction And Fantasy, Sept 1953, No 1.*
Illustrator not credited.

b. Science Fiction Monthly (Australian), No 7, undated (March 1956).

45. "The Gun" (4650 words)

A space-faring race lands on a devastated Earth. They find an automatic self-repairing gun protecting Earth's archives.

a. Planet Stories, Sept 1952.*
Illustrated by Herman Vestal.

b. Science Fiction Monthly (Australian), No 12, undated (Aug 1956).

46. "The Hanging Stranger" (5300 words)

In Pikeville, no one but Ed Loyce notices a body hanging from a lamp post. Everyone else has come under the psychic control of insectile aliens. The hanging body is a trap to expose the random few who have not yet been subjugated.

a. Science Fiction Adventures, Dec 1953.*
Illustrated by Smith.

47. "His Predictions"

Non-Fiction.

A number of predictions about the future by various people all under the same title.

a. THE BOOK OF PREDICTIONS, Ed by David Wallechinsky, Morrow, New York ($12.95), 1981.*

48. "Holy Quarrel" (6000 words)

The Genux-B computer has declared a state of red alert and plans to obliterate Northern California. Frantic repairmen learn only that the computer wishes to destroy one Herb Sousa and his chain of gum-ball machines. Genux-B believes the gum-balls are alive and that Herb Sousa is the devil incarnate.

a. Worlds of Tomorrow, May 1966.*
Illustrated by Adkins.

b. (as "Quel Agresseur?") [French], Galaxie, New Series, Nov 1967, No 43.

c. (as "F.B.I. Non Risponde") [Italian], Urania No 452, 1967.
   Translator: B Russo.

45.a.   48.a.

49. **"The Hood Maker"** (5400 words)

**Telepaths have taken oven the modern and evolved method of adminis-
tering loyalty oaths. They can read anyone, anytime, except for those
wearing a thin alloy strip around their heads.**

a. Imagination, June 1955.*
   Illustrated by W E Terry (?).

50. **"Human Is"** (4800 words)

**A cold and abrasive toxicologist is ambushed on an alien planet. His
mind is emptied and replaced by that of a creature who wishes to infil-
trate the Earth.**

*"To me, this story states my early conclusions as to what is human. I have
not really changed my view since I wrote this story, back in the fifties. It's
not what you look like, or what planet you were born on. It's how kind you
are. The quality of kindness, to me, distinguishes us from rocks and sticks
and metal, and will forever, whatever shape we take, wherever we go,
whatever we become. For me, 'Human Is' is my credo. May it be yours."*
—PKD

    a. Startling Stories, Winter 1955.*

    b. THE BEST OF PHILIP K. DICK, Ballantine: 25359, 1977, paper.*

    c. (as "Définir L'Humain") [French], LE LIVRE D'OR DE LA SCIENCE-FICTION: PHILIP K. DICK, Ed by Marcel Thaon, Presses Pocket: 5051, 1979, paper.*

51. "If There Were No Benny Cemoli" (5500 words)

Manuscript title "Had There Never Been A Benny Cemoli".

The Proxmen rebuilding war-torn Earth want to prosecute its leaders for war crimes. Benny Cemoli would be the biggest catch of all, if they could just find him.

"I have always believed that at least half the famous people in history never existed. You invent what you need to invent. Perhaps even Karl Marx was invented, the product of some hack writer. In which case—"—PKD

    a. Galaxy, Dec 1963.*
       Illustrated by Lutjens.

    b. (as "Se Non Ci Fosse Benny Cemoli") [Italian], Galassia No 44, 1964.

    c. THE EIGHTH GALAXY READER, Ed by Frederick Pohl, Doubleday, Garden City ($3.95), 1965.*

    d. (as "Si Cemoli N'Existait Pas . . .") [French], Galaxie, New Series, Feb 1966, No 22.

    e. THE PRESERVING MACHINE, Ace: 67800, 1969, paper.*

    f. (as "Se Non Ci Fosse Benny Cemoli") [Italian], LE VOCI DOPO, Fanucci, Futuro 26, 1976, paper.*

    g. THE BEST OF PHILIP K. DICK, Ballantine: 25359, 1977, paper.*

    h. (as "Si No Existiera Benny Cemoli") [Spanish], LA MAQUINA PRESERV-ADORA, Edhasa: 23, 1978, paper.*

52. "If You Find This World Bad, You Should See Some Of The Others"

Non-Fiction.

Given at the 2nd Festival International de la Science-Fiction de Metz on 24 Sept 1977.

    a. (as "Si Vous Trouvés Ce Monde Mauvais, Vous Devriez En Voir Quelques Autres") [French], L'ANNÉE 1977-1978 DE LA S.F. ET DU FANTASTIQUE, Ed by Jacques Goimard, Julliard, 1978, paper.

53. "The Impossible Planet" (3000 words)

Earth has been proved to be a mythical planet, but an old, old woman is willing to pay good money to be taken there.

    a. Imagination, Oct 1953.*

    b. A HANDFUL OF DARKNESS, Rich & Cowan, London, 1955.*

c. (as "De Onmogelijke Planeet") [Dutch], EEN HANDVOL DUISTERNIS, A W Bruna: 1100, 1968, paper.*

d. SPACE ODYSSEYS, Ed by Brian W Aldiss, Orbit: 816 (75p), 1974, paper.

e. (as "De Onmogelijke Planeet") [Dutch], DE ONMOGELIJKE PLANEET, A W Bruna: SF 40, 1976, paper.*

f. (as "Il Pianeta Impossibile") [Italian], ENCICLOPEDIA FS No 1, Fannucci, Rome (L 7500), 1978, paper.
Translator: R Rambelli.

g. (as "La Planete Impossibile") [French], LE LIVRE D'OR DE LA SCIENCE-FICTION: PHILIP K. DICK, Ed by Marcel Thaon, Presses Pocket: 5051, 1979, paper.*

h. (as "La Planete Impossible") [French], L'ANNÉE 1978-1979 DE LA SCIENCE-FICTION ET DU FANTASTIQUE, Ed by Jacques Goimard, Julliard, 1979, paper.*

54. "Impostor" (6000 words)

Spence Olham is essential to the project that may win the war against the outspacers. Terran Security thinks Olham may not be the man he believes himself to be.

*"Here was my first story on the topic of: Am I a human? Or am I just programmed to believe I am human? When you consider that I wrote this back in 1953, it was, if I may say so, a pretty damn good new idea in sf. Of course, by now I've done it to death. But the theme still preoccupies me. It's an important theme because it forces us to ask: What **is** a human? And—what isn't?"—PKD*

54.a.

54.l.

a. Astounding, June 1953.*
    Illustrated by Pawelka.

b. Astounding (British), Nov 1953.

c. A HANDFUL OF DARKNESS, Rich & Cowan, London, 1955.*

d. SCIENCE FICTION TERROR TALES, Ed by Groff Conklin, Gnome Press, New York ($3.50), 1955.*

e. BEST SF 2, Ed by Edmund Crispin, Faber & Faber, London (15/-), 1956.

f. (as "Imposter") THE END OF THE WORLD, Ed by Donald A Wollheim, Ace: S-183 ($0.25), 1956, paper.

g. (as "L'Imposteur") [French], Galaxie, New Series, Aug 1964, No 4.

h. UNTRAVELLED WORLDS, Ed by Alan F Barter and R Wilson, Macmillan (7/6), 1966, paper.

i. THE METAL SMILE, Ed by Damon Knight, Belmont: B60-082 ($0.60), 1968, paper.*
    The contents page lists "Impostor" but the story title and running heads say "Imposter".

j. (as "De Bedrieger") [Dutch], EEN HANDVOL DUISTERNIS, A W Bruna: 1100, 1968, paper.*

k. DARK STARS, Ed by Robert Silverberg, Ballantine: 01796 ($0.95), 1969, paper.*

l. (as   ) [Japanese], Title and Publisher—?, 1970.*
    Book contains "Impostor," and "The Leech" by R Sheckley. This is a hardcover book, somewhat larger than most American hardcover books, with a beautiful dustjacket. Unfortunately, except for the story titles and author's names the rest is in Japanese.

m. (as "Impostore") [Italian], Nova SF No 13, 1971.
    Translator: U Malaguti.

n. THE ASTOUNDING-ANALOG READER, VOLUME TWO, Ed by Harry Harrison and Brian W. Aldiss, Doubleday, Garden City ($7.95), 1973.*

o. (as "De Bedrieger") [Dutch], DE ONMOGELIJKE PLANEET, A W Bruna: SF 40, 1976, paper.*

p. THE BEST OF PHILIP K. DICK, Ballantine: 25359, 1977, paper.*

q. SOULS IN METAL, Ed by Michael Ashley, St Martin's, New York ($6.95), 1977.*

r. (as "Dubbelganger") [Dutch], SPRONG NAAR OMEGA, Ed by Albert van Hageland, DAP Reinaert, 1978, paper.

s. THE ARBOR HOUSE TREASURY OF MODERN SCIENCE FICTION, Ed by Robert Silverberg and Martin H Greenberg, Arbor House ($19.95), 1980.*

55. **"The Indefatigable Frog"** (3400 words)

Two eccentric scientists find their relationship strained in a test of Zeno's Paradox. Can logic and the laws of physics both be right?

   a. Fantastic Story Magazine, July 1953.*

   b. A HANDFUL OF DARKNESS, Rich & Cowan, London, 1955.*

   c. (as "L'Infatigable Grenouille") [French], LES DÉLIRES DIVERGENTS DE PHILIP K. DICK, Ed by Alain Doremieux, Casterman, Paris, 1979.*

56. **"The Infinites"** (7600 words)

A wave of radiation causes rapid evolution of the crew and experimental animals on a small exploration vessel.

   a. Planet Stories, May 1953.*
     Illustrated by Kelly Freas.

   b. Science Fiction Monthly (Australian), No 18, undated (Feb 1957).

   c. (as "Les Infinis") [French], LES MEILLEURS RECITS DE PLANET STORIES, Ed by Jacques Sadoul, J'ai Lu, 1975, paper.

56.a.

57.a.

57. Interviews

    a. "Vertex Interviews Philip K. Dick", conducted by Arthur Byron Cover, Vertex, Feb 1974, Vol 1 No 6.*
Reprinted in German in Science Fiction Times Special Issue No 1: PHILIP K. DICK—MATERIALIEN, 1976.*

    b. Untitled, by Tony Hiss in "The Talk Of The Town" column in the New Yorker, 27 Jan 1975 and 3 Feb 1975.*

57.a. — interior.

    c. "An Interview With Philip K. Dick", conducted by Daniel DePrez, Science Fiction Review, Aug 1976, No 19.*

    d. "An Interview With America's Most Brilliant Science-Fiction Writer", conducted by Joe Vilale, The Aquarian, 11 Oct-18 Oct 1978.*

    e. "A Rebrousse-DICK" [French], conducted by Jerome Piroue, Point Final, No 3, 1979.*
Published in Switzerland.

    f. "Philip K. Dick In Walkie Talkie Dam 2001" [German], Nova 2001, No 1/2, Jan-Feb 1979.
Selected parts of interview in item g below.

    g. "Interview Mit Philip K. Dick" [German], conducted by Werner Fuchs and Uwe Anton, Science Fiction Times, No 146, April-May-June 1979.

    h. Untitled, conducted by Charles Platt, DREAM MAKERS, Ed by Charles Platt, Berkley: 04668 ($2.75), 1980, paper.*

    i. "Horselover Fat And The New Messiah", conducted by John Boonstra, The Hartford Advocate, 22 April 1981.*

58. "James P. Crow" (7000 words)

Humans are placed in the same inferior position relative to robots that Blacks once occupied with respect to whites after the Reconstruction.

   a. Planet Stories, May 1954.*
      Illustrated by Ed Emshwiller.

59. "Jon's World"

The purpose of the first time trip to the past is to obtain the lost secret of the mechanical brain. A little boy foresees the ensuing paradox and the changes that would ensue if the trip should fail.

   a. TIME TO COME, Ed by August Derleth, Farrar Straus & Young, New York ($3.50), 1954.*
      Two piece binding with black cloth on the spine and blue marbled paper boards. Lettering is in white on the spine except that the title is yellow. No date on the title page. "First printing, 1954" is on the copyright page.

60. "The King Of The Elves" (7100 words)

Because of his kindness and generosity, a gas-station attendant is chosen to lead the fight against the trolls.

"This story, of course, is fantasy, not SF. Originally it had a downbeat ending on it, but Horace Gold, the editor who bought it, carefully explained to me that prophecy always came true; if it didn't ipso facto it wasn't prophecy. I guess, then, there can be no such thing as a false prophet; 'false prophet' is an oxymoron."—PKD

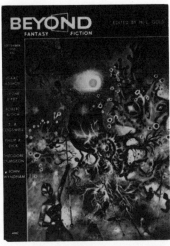

60.a.   61.a.

   a. Beyond Fantasy Fiction, Sept 1953.*
      Illustrated by Barth.

   b. THE GOLDEN MAN, Ed by Mark Hurst, Berkley: 04288, 1980, paper.*

61. **"The Last Of The Masters"** (10600 words)

The anarchist uprising had destroyed all of the world's armies, but Bors had survived two hundred years in secret, and planned to rebuild his own fighting force to conquer the world.

"Now I show trust of robot as leader, a robot who is the suffering servant, which is to say a form of Christ. Leader as servant of man: leader who should be dispensed with—perhaps. An ambiguity hangs over the morality of this story. Should we have a leader or should we think for ourselves? Obviously the latter, in principle. But—sometimes there lies a gulf between what is theoretically right and that which is practical. It's interesting that I would trust a robot and not an android. Perhaps it's because a robot does not try to deceive you as to what it is."—PKD

a. Orbit Science Fiction, Nov-Dec 1954, No 5.*
    Not illustrated.

b. SPACE STATION 42 AND OTHER STORIES (Australian), Jubilee Publications Pty Ltd, Sydney, undated (No 212, March 1958).*
    This is the second issue of the "Satellite Series", whose numbering started with No 211.

c. THE GOLDEN MAN, Ed by Mark Hurst, Berkley: 04288, 1980, paper.*

62. **Letters**

Although no attempt has been made to trace all of Philip K Dick's published letters, a sampling of readily accessible letters is included for those interested.

a. The Alien Critic, No 6, Aug 1973.*

b. SF Commentary, No 9, Feb 1970.

c. SF Commentary, No 17, Nov 1970.*

d. SF Commentary, No 39, Nov 1973.*

e. Vector 67-68, Spring 1974.*

f. Scintillation, No 12, March 1977.*

g. Science-Fiction Studies, No 14, Vol 5 Part 1, March 1978.*

h. Science Fiction Review, No 39, Vol 10 No 2, Summer 1981.*

63. **"The Little Black Box"** (9900 words)

It is only natural that the telepaths are the first to fall under the influence of Mercerism; the new religion of empathy. The government would like to ask them where the empathy boxes take them and just who is Wilbur Mercer?

"I made use of this story when I wrote my novel DO ANDROIDS DREAM OF ELECTRIC SHEEP? Actually, the idea is better put forth in the story. Here, a religion is regarded as a menace to all political systems; therefore it, too, is a kind of political system, perhaps even an ultimate one. The concept of **caritas** *(or* **agape***) shows up in my writing as the key to the authentic*

human. The android, which is the unauthentic human, the mere reflex machine, is unable to experience empathy. In this story it is never clear whether Mercer is an invader from some other world. But he must be; in a sense all religious leaders are . . . but not from another planet as such."
—PKD

a. Worlds of Tomorrow, Aug 1964.*
   Illustrated by Schelling.

b. (as "Loue Soit Mercer") [French], Galaxie, New Series, June 1967, No 38.

c. THE GOLDEN MAN, Ed by Mark Hurst, Berkley: 04288, 1980, paper.*

64. "The Little Movement" (3700 words)
A megalomaniacal conspiracy of animate tin soldiers is thwarted by a homely underground organization of toys.

a. Fantasy & Science Fiction, Nov 1952.*
   Not illustrated.

b. A HANDFUL OF DARKNESS, Rich & Cowan, London, 1955.*

c. (as "Minirevolte") [French], Fiction, May 1967, No 162.

d. (as "Minibattaglia") [Italian], Urania No 473, 1967.
   Translator: B della Frattina.

e. THE EUREKA YEARS: BOUCHER-MCCOMAS F & SF, 1949-54, Ed by Annette McComas, Bantam.
   Forthcoming.

65. "A Little Something For Us Tempunauts"
On the first time excursion, three voyagers become trapped in a closed time loop. In an entropic system, they are exhaustedly forced to examine and reexamine the inevitability of their own deaths.
"In this story I felt a vast weariness over the space program, which had thrilled us so at the start—especially the first lunar landing—and then had been forgotten and virtually shut down, a relic of history. I wondered, if time travel became a 'program,' would it suffer the same fate? Or was there an even worse possibility latent in it, within the very nature of the paradoxes of time travel?"—PKD

a. FINAL STAGE, Ed by Edward L Ferman and Barry N Malzberg, Charterhouse, New York ($7.95), 1974.*

b. THE BEST SCIENCE FICTION OF THE YEAR NO 4, Ed by Terry Carr, Ballantine: 24529 ($1.95), 1975, paper.*

c. (as "Algo Para Nosotros Temponautas") [Spanish], ULTIMA ETAPA, Ed by Edward L Ferman and Barry N Malzberg, Editorial Bruguera, 1976, paper.*

  d. (as "Een Kleinigheid Voor Ons Temponauten") [Dutch], SCIENCE
     FICTION-VERHALEN 7, Ed by Terry Carr, Het Spectrum: Prisma 1755,
     1976, paper.

  e. THE BEST OF PHILIP K. DICK, Ballantine: 25359, 1977, paper.*

  f. (as "Noi Temponauti") [Italian], Robot No 15, 1977.
     Translator: A Luraschi.

  g. (as "Temponauti") [Italian], Oscar SF No 815, 1977, paper.
     Translator: H Brinis.

66. "The Lucky Dog Pet Store"
Non-Fiction.

  a. Foundation, No 17, Sept 1979.*
     As a contribution to the column "The Profession Of Science Fiction"
     number XVII. Foundation assigned the title.

  b. (as "Introduction") THE GOLDEN MAN, Ed by Mark Hurst, Berkley:
     04288, 1980, paper.*
     Minor changes.

67. "Man, Android And Machine"
Non-Fiction.

  a. SCIENCE FICTION AT LARGE, Ed by Peter Nicholls, Gollancz, London
     (£5.95), 1976.*

68. "Martians Come In Clouds" (3500 words)
A little boy detects one of the ethereal invaders from Mars.

  a. Fantastic Universe, June-July 1954.*
     Not illustrated.

69. "Meddler" (4400 words)
**The Council cannot resist sending the time-dip into the future, though
each attempt seems to result in an accelerating spiral of dire conse-
quences.**

*"Within the beautiful lurks the ugly; you can see in this rather crude story
the germ of my whole theme that nothing is what it seems. This story should
be read as a trial run on my part; I was just beginning to grasp that obvious
form and latent form are not the same thing. As Heraclitus said in fragment
54: 'Latent structure is master of obvious structure,' and out of this comes
the later more sophisticated Platonic dualism between the phenomenal
world and the real but invisible realm of forms lying behind it. I may be
reading too much into this simple-minded early story, but at least I was
beginning to see in a dim way what I later saw so clearly; in fragment 123,
Heraclitus said, 'The nature of things is in the habit of concealing itself,' and
therein lies it all."—PKD*

a. Future, Oct 1954.*
   Illustrated by Virgil Finlay.

b. (as "Touché À Tout") [French], Satellite, Dec 1958, No 12.

c. THE GOLDEN MAN, Ed by Mark Hurst, Berkley: 04288, 1980, paper.*

69.a.

69.a. — interior.

70. "Memories Found In A Bill From A Small Animal Vet"
Non-Fiction.
PKD talks about a friend, mentor and fellow-writer, Anthony Boucher, and his death.

a. The Real World, No 5, Feb-March 1976.*

71. "The Minority Report" (16700 words)
The pre-crime plan has wrested control of the police back from the Army. It involves pre-cogs and the detainment of citizens who intend to commit crimes before they can act. Anderton, the commissioner of pre-crime, intercepts a report that he is going to become a murderer. The report must be false, a plot. There must be an alternative or pre-crime is invalidated.

a. Fantastic Universe, Jan 1956.*
   Not illustrated.

b. THE VARIABLE MAN, Ace: D-261, 1957, paper.*

c. (as "Rapporto Di Minoranza") [Italian], Urania No 385, 1965.
   Translator: B della Frattina.

d. (as "Het Minderheidsrapport") [Dutch], EEN SWIBBEL VOOR DAG EN NACHT, A W Bruna: 1295, 1969, paper.*

e. (as "Rapporto Di Minoranza") [Italian], L'UOMO VARIABILE, Fanucci: Futuro 45, 1979, paper.*
   Translators: M Nati and T Tagliamonte.

71.a.

80.a.

72. **"Misadjustment"** (7500 words)
    Males with mutant psi-powers form a threat to a stabilized society, so females separate out and control the dangerous ones.

    a. Science Fiction Quarterly, Feb 1957.*
       Illustrated by Ed Emshwiller.

    b. (as "Mefiez-Vous Les Uns Des Autres") [French], LE LIVRE D'OR DE LA SCIENCE-FICTION: PHILIP K. DICK, Ed by Marcel Thaon, Presses Pocket: 5051, 1979, paper.*

73. **"The Mold Of Yancy"** (8200 words)
    A cult of personality is built up around an imaginary video figure in order to control the tastes, ideals and habits of society.
    "Obviously, Yancy is based on President Eisenhower. During his reign we all were worrying about the man-in-the-gray-flannel-suit problem; we feared that the entire country was turning into one person and a whole lot of clones. (Although in those days the word 'clone' was unknown to us.) I liked this story enough to use it as the basis for my novel THE PENULTIMATE TRUTH; in particular the part where everything the government tells you is a lie. I still like that part; I mean, I still believe it's so. Watergate, of course, bore the basic idea of this story out." – PKD

b. THE SECOND WORLD OF IF, Ed by James L Quinn and Eve Wulff, Quinn ($0.50), 1958, paper.*
Magazine format.

c. THE GOLDEN MAN, Ed by Mark Hurst, Berkley: 04288, 1980, paper.*

72.a. — interior.

74. **"Mr. Spaceship"** (10700 words)
Automatically controlled Terran ships cannot break the blockade. A more aware control system is devised; one with a living brain. Its higher centers are supposedly inactivated, but it seems to fuction in an odd manner.

a. Imagination, Jan 1953.*
Illustrated by W E Terry (?).

75. **"Nanny"** (7000 words)
Robot nursemaids are programmed combatively. Each new model is more formidable than the last, and more expensive.

a. Startling Stories, Spring 1955.*

b. THE BOOK OF PHILIP K. DICK, DAW: 44, 1973, paper.*

c. [Italian], I DIFENSORI DELLA TERRA, Fanucci: Futuro 34, 1977, paper.*

76. **"Naziism And The High Castle"**
Non-Fiction.
PKD remarks on racism and the de-mythification of National Socialism.

a. Niekas, No 9, Sept 1964.*

77. **"The Nixon Crowd"**
Non-Fiction.

    a. SF Commentary No 39, Nov 1973.

    b. (as "Die Nixon-Bande") [German], Science Fiction Times, No 134, 1974.

    c. (as "Die Nixon-Bande") [German], Science Fiction Times, Special Issue No 1: PHILIP K. DICK—MATERIALIEN, 1976.*

78. **"Not By Its Cover"** (2500 words)
In which the philosophy and preservative qualities of wub-fur are discussed.

*"Here I presented what used to be a wish on my part: that the Bible was true. Obviously, I was at a sort of halfway point between doubt and faith. Years later I'm still in that position; I'd **like** the Bible to be true, but—well, maybe if it isn't we can make it so. But, alas, it's going to take plenty of work to do it."—PKD*

    a. Famous Science Fiction, Summer 1968.

    b. THE GOLDEN MAN, Ed by Mark Hurst, Berkley: 04288, 1980, paper.*

79. **"Notes Made Late At Night By A Weary SF Writer"**
Non-Fiction.
Some of PKD's thoughts on writing SF and the problem of making a living at it.

    a. Eternity Science Fiction, Old Series, No 1, July 1972.*

80. **"Novelty Act"** (12900 words)
Congregating in socialistic condos, Americans worship their president's wife and hope to entertain her at the White House's amateur hour. This is one of the three options open to them: conform, perform or emigrate to Mars.

    a. Fantastic, Feb 1964.*
    Illustrated by Lutjens.

    b. THE HUMAN EQUATION, Ed by William F Nolan, Sherbourne, Los Angeles ($7.50), 1971.*

81. **"Null-0"** (4000 words)
A small group of mutants, anomic and paranoid and thus perfectly logical, scheme to maximize entropy.

    a. If, Dec 1958.*
    Illustrated by Ed Emshwiller.

82. **"Of Withered Apples"** (3100 words)
In the realm of horror, an old and evil tree reproduces itself in the body of a young woman.

    a. Cosmos Science Fiction and Fantasy, July 1954, No 4.*
    Not illustrated.

83. "Oh, To Be A Blobel!" (6000 words)

Manuscript title "Well, See, There Were These Blobels".

George Munster was biologically transformed into a spy for the Blobel-Terran conflict. Only partially recidivated, he is having trouble holding down a job and supporting his family, who are also having certain identity crises.

"Here I nailed down the ultimate meaningless irony of war: the human turns into a Blobel, and the Blobel, his enemy, turns into a human, and there it all is, the futility, the black humor, the stupidity. And in the story they all wind up happy."—PKD

81.a.   83.a.

a. Galaxy, Feb 1964.*
   Illustrated by Gray Morrow.

b. (as "Quelle Chance D'Etre Un Blobel!") [French], Galaxie, New Series, Nov 1964, No 7.

c. WORLD'S BEST SCIENCE FICTION: 1965, Ed by Donald A Wollheim and Terry Carr, Ace: G-551 ($0.50), 1965, paper.*

d. THE PRESERVING MACHINE, Ace: 67800, 1969, paper.*

e. INFINITE JESTS, Ed by Robert Silverberg, Chilton, Philadelphia ($5.95), 1974.*

f. (as "Oh, Sur Un Blobell!") [Spanish], ANTOLOGIA DE NOVELAS DE AN-TICIPACION—VOLUMEN QUINTO, Ediciones Acervo, Barcelona, 1975 (?).

g. THE BEST OF PHILIP K. DICK, Ballantine: 25359, 1977, paper.*

h. (as "Essere Un Blobel") [Italian], I DIFENSORI DELLA TERRA, Fanucci: Futuro 34, 1977, paper.*

    i. (as "O, Was Ik Maar Een Blobel!") [Dutch], JOKERS UIT HET HEELAL, Ed by Robert Silverberg, Luitingh, 1977, paper (?).

    j. (as "Quien Fuera Medubel!") [Spanish], EN LA TIERRA SOMBRIA, Edhasa: 26, 1978, paper.*

    k. GALAXY: THIRTY YEARS OF INNOVATIVE SCIENCE FICTION, Ed by Frederik Pohl, Martin H Greenberg and Joseph D Olander, Playboy Press, Chicago ($10.95), 1980.*
       Also includes a foreword by Philip K. Dick.

    l. ALIENS, Ed by Gardner R Dozois and Jack M Dann, Pocket: 83155 ($2.25), 1980, paper.*

    m. FREDERIK POHL'S FAVORITE STORIES, Ed by Frederik Pohl. Forthcoming. To be published as a trade paperback by Berkley.

84. "An Old Snare"
Verse.

A short poem, about 12 lines as Dick remembers.

    a. A CHILD'S HAT, Ed by Ward J Gulyas, Published by the editor, 1966, paper.

85. "An Open Letter To Joanna Russ"
Non-Fiction.

    a. Vertex, Oct 1974.*

86. "Out In The Garden" (3100 words)
A mother, a father, a child, a voice,
A line from Yeats and a line from Joyce.

    a. Fantasy Fiction, Aug 1953.*
       Illustrated by Kelly Freas.

    b. SATAN'S PETS, Ed by Vic Ghidalia, Manor: 75-478 ($0.75), 1972, paper.

87. "Pay For The Printer" (6100 words)
Civilization is mostly destroyed. The survivors try to maintain their lives by having the extraterrestrial Biltungs copy Earth's vital artifacts, such as toasters and ceramic lamps.

    a. Satellite Science Fiction, Oct 1956.*
       Not illustrated.

    b. THE PRESERVING MACHINE, Ace: 67800, 1969, paper.*

    c. (as "De Dood Van De Biltongs") [Dutch], DE ONMOGELIJKE PLANEET, A W Bruna: SF 40, 1976, paper.*

    d. (as " 'Diffidate Dalle Imitazioni!' ") [Italian], Fantascienza No 2, 1976. Translator: M Nati.

e. (as " 'Diffidate Dalle Imitazioni!' ") [Italian], LE VOCI DI DOPO, Fanucci: Futuro 26, 1976, paper.*

f. (as "El Precio De La Imitacion") [Spanish], EN LA TIERRA SOMBRIA, Edhasa: 26, 1978, paper.*

g. (as "Payer L'Imprimeur!") [French], LE LIVRE D'OR DE LA SCIENCE-FICTION: PHILIP K. DICK, Ed by Marcel Thaon, Presses Pocket: 5051, 1979, paper.*

88. "Paycheck" (13000 words)

The great battle of society pits the government against the corporations. The Security Police want to find out what was wiped from Jenning's mind in the two years he worked for Rethrick Construction, and so does he. His only advantage will be his former control of the time-scoop.

"How much is a key to a bus locker worth? One day it's worth 25¢, the next day thousands of dollars. In this story, I got to thinking that there are times in our lives when having a dime to make a phone call spells the difference between life and death. Keys, small change, maybe a theater ticket—how about a parking receipt for a Jaguar? All I had to do was link this idea up with time travel to see how the small and useless, under the wise eyes of a time traveler, might signify a great deal more. He would know when that dime might save your life. And, back in the past again, he might prefer that dime to any amount of money, no matter how large."—PKD

a. Imagination, June 1953.*
   Illustrated by W E Terry.

b. THE BEST OF PHILIP K. DICK, Ballantine: 25359, 1977, paper.*

89. "Piper In The Woods" (6500 words)

Technicians working on a bucolic asteroid become convinced they have been transformed into plants.

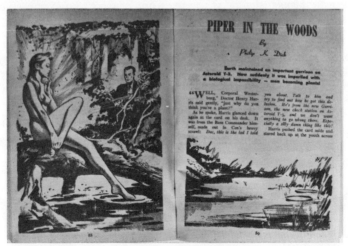

89.a. — interior.

a. Imagination, Feb 1953.*
Illustrated by W E Terry (?).
"Introducing The Author" in this issue features Philip K Dick and contains a photo and 250 words of biography by Philip K Dick; all found on the inside front cover.

b. Popular Science Fiction (Australian), Vol 1 No 2, undated (Nov 1953).

c. OTHER WORLDS, OTHER TIMES, Ed by Sam Moskowitz and Roger Elwood, Macfadden: 75-238 ($0.75), 1969, paper.*

d. (as "Musici Nei Boschi") [Italian], Nova SF No 30, 1975.
Translator: W Saudi.

90. "Planet For Transients" (4800 words)
Parts of this story were adapted for DEUS IRAE.
Mutants adapted to radioactivity are the rule, not the exception, on Earth after the Atomic War. Some normal men exist in caves, but they must leave Earth to survive.

a. Fantastic Universe, Oct-Nov 1953.*
Not illustrated.

b. A HANDFUL OF DARKNESS, Rich & Cowan, London, 1955.*

c. (as "Passanten") [Dutch], EEN HANDVOL DUISTERNIS, A W Bruna: 1100, 1968, paper.*

91. "The Pre-Persons"
If you are less than twelve years old, or if you are unable to solve algebraic problems in your head, you legally have no soul; you can be aborted. Your mother makes a phone call and up drives the truck from the pound. . . .
"In this I incurred the absolute hate of Joanna Russ who wrote me the nastiest letter I've ever received; at one point she said she usually offered to beat up people (she didn't use the word 'people') who expressed opinions such as this. I admit that this story amounts to special pleading, and I am sorry to offend those who disagree with me about abortion on demand. I also got some unsigned hate mail, some of it not from individuals but from organizations promoting abortion on demand. Well, I have always managed to get myself into hot water. Sorry, people. But for the pre-person's sake I am not sorry. I stand where I stand: 'Hier steh' Ich; Ich kann nicht anders,' as Martin Luther is supposed to have said."—PKD

a. Fantasy & Science Fiction, Oct 1974.*

b. (as "Les Pre-Humains") [French], Nouvelles Frontières, No 1, 1975.

c. (as "Les Pre-Humains") [French], LES DÉLIRES DIVERGENTS DE PHILIP K. DICK, Ed by Alain Doremieux, Casterman, Paris, 1979.*

d. THE GOLDEN MAN, Ed by Mark Hurst, Berkeley: 04288, 1980, paper.*

92. **"Precious Artifact"** (5900 words)

By disguising themselves as Terrans, the Proxmen hope to get engineer Biskle to reconstruct the Earth for them, just as he has done on Mars.

*"This story utilized a peculiar logic which I generally employ, which Professor Patricia Warrick pointed out to me. First you have Y. Then you do a cybernetics flipflop and you have null-Y. Okay, now you reverse it again and have null-null-Y. Okay, the question is: Does null-null-Y equal Y³? Or is it a deepening of null-Y? In this story, what appears to be the case is Y but we find out the opposite is true (null-Y). But then **that** turns out not to be true, so are we back to Y? Professor Warrick says that my logic winds up with Y equals null-Y. I don't agree, but I'm not sure what I do wind up with. Whatever it is, in terms of logic, it is contained in this particular story. Either I've invented a whole new logic or, ahem, I'm not playing with a full deck."* — PKD

    a. Galaxy, Oct 1964.*
       Not illustrated.

    b. (as "Il Gatto") [Italian], Urania No 372, 1965.
       Translator: B della Frattina.

    c. (as "Simulacre") [French], Galaxie, New Series, March 1966, No 23.

    d. (as "Precieuse Relique") [French], LES DÉLIRES DIVERGENTS DE PHILIP K. DICK, Ed by Alain Doremieux, Casterman, Paris, 1979.*

    e. THE GOLDEN MAN, Ed by Mark Hurst, Berkley: 04288, 1980, paper.*

93. **"A Present For Pat"** (7100 words)

A Ganymedean god turns out to be a cop from a higher dimensional continuum.

    a. Startling Stories, Jan 1954.*

    b. Startling Stories (British), No 17, undated (March 1954).*

    c. S-F Yearbook, A Treasury Of Science Fiction, No 4, 1970.*

    d. THE BOOK OF PHILIP K. DICK, DAW: 44, 1973, paper.*

    e. (as "Un Regalo Per Pat") [Italian], I DIFENSORI DELLA TERRA, Fanucci: Futuro 34, 1977, paper.*

94. **"The Preserving Machine"** (3800 words)

Musical creations are given objective reality in animal form. They then immediately proceed to subjectivise themselves.

    a. Fantasy & Science Fiction, June 1953.*
       Not illustrated.

    b. (as "La Machine À Sauver La Musique") [French], Univers, No 12, 1953 (?).

    c. A HANDFUL OF DARKNESS, Rich & Cowan, London, 1955.*

d. THE PRESERVING MACHINE, Ace: 67800, 1969, paper.*

e. (as "Conservazione Della Specie") [Italian], Nova SF No 12, 1970.

f. THE SCIENCE FICTION BESTIARY, Ed by Robert Silverberg, Thomas Nelson, New York ($5.95), 1971.*

g. (as "La Macchina Salvamusica") [Italian], LE VOCI DI DOPO, Fanuuci: Futuro 26, 1976, paper.*

h. (as "La Maquina Preservadora") [Spanish], LA MAQUINA PRESERVADORA, Edhasa: 23, 1978, paper.*

95. "Prize Ship" (7750 words)

The Terrans capture a new ship in the Ganymedean War. When they test it, the vessel takes them to places in which the universe has contracted and expanded.

a. Thrilling Wonder Stories, Winter 1954.*
Illustrated by Virgil Finlay.

96. "Progeny" (6200 words)

The Skinner-box method of raising children is developed to its ultimate extension.

86.a.

98.a.

a. If, Nov 1954.*
Illustrated by Ralph Castenir.

b. A HANDFUL OF DARKNESS, Rich & Cowan, London, 1955.*

c. (as "Kroost") [Dutch], EEN HANDVOL DUISTERNIS, A W Bruna: 1100, 1968, paper.*

d. (as "Progeniture") [French], Fiction, Oct 1972, No 226.

e. SCHOOL AND SOCIETY THROUGH SCIENCE FICTION, Ed by Joseph D Olander, Martin H Greenberg and Patricia S Warrick, Rand-McNally, Chicago ($5.95), 1974, paper.*

f. MARRIAGE AND THE FAMILY THROUGH SCIENCE FICTION, Ed by Val Clear, Patricia S Warrick, Martin H Greenberg and Joseph D Olander, St Martin's, New York ($12.95), 1976.

97. "Project: Earth" (8000 words)

The old man has been working interminably on his book; all the facts about everyone in the world. He also has a cage full of tiny people with antennae.

a. Imagination, Dec 1953.*
Illustrated by W E Terry (?).

98. "Project Plowshare" (67500 words)

Published as THE ZAP GUN.

Lars Powderdry is a mystic in a cold war world. He enters a trance and returns with new weapon designs. Some are plowshared, or disguised as innocuous items. Wes-Bloc designer Lars has an opposite number working for Peep-East; thus the status quo is maintained. But certain tensions are building from within.

a. Worlds Of Tomorrow, sr2, Nov 1965, Jan 1966.*
Illustrated by Gray Morrow.

b. (as "Les Convertisseurs D'Armes") [French], Galaxie, New Series, sr2, Nov 1968, Dec 1968, No 54, 55.

99. "Prominent Author" (6400 words)

The jiffy-scuttler is a quick way to and from work, but it develops some thin spots in the fourth dimension. Henry Ellis makes some unusual contacts through the jiffy-scuttler who regard him as a very important person.

a. If, May 1954.*
Illustrated by Paul Orban.

b. If (British), Vol 1 No 10, undated (Aug 1954).

c. A HANDFUL OF DARKNESS, Rich & Cowan, London, 1955.*

d. (as "Un Anteur Eminent") [French], Fiction, May 1969, No 185.

"Psi-Man"

See "Psi-Man Heal My Child!"

100. "Psi-Man Heal My Child!" (8000 words)

The Earth is a twisted ruin and the remnants of the population live in underground bunkers. Only the psis live on the surface. Two questions about them remain unresolved: Can the Psi-men really help the humans, and will they even be asked?

a. Imaginative Tales, Nov 1955.*

b. (as "Psi-Man") THE BOOK OF PHILIP K. DICK, DAW: 44, 1973, paper.*

c. (as "Psi") [Italian], I DEFENSORI DELLA TERRA, Fanucci: Futuro 34, 1977, paper.*

101. "Rautavaara's Case"

Aliens perform theological experimentation in a damaged human brain.

a. Omni, Oct 1980.*

102. "Recall Mechanism" (5900 words)

A government planner has a phobia about heights. His latent psionic ability is warning him of his death at the hands of a mirror-image neurotic.

a. If, July 1959.*
Illustrated by Ed Emshwiller.

b. (as "Souvenir-Ecran") [French], LE LIVRE D'OR DE LA SCIENCE-FICTION: PHILIP K. DICK, Ed by Marcel Thaon, Presses Pocket: 5051, 1979, paper.*

"Retreat From Rigel"

See "Tony And The Beetles"

103. "Retreat Syndrome" (6000 words)

The revolt on Ganymede is failing because of what John Cupertino told his wife. So, he decides to kill her again . . . and again.

a. Worlds Of Tomorrow, Jan 1965.*
Illustrated by Gray Morrow.

b. (as "Syndrome De Retraite") [French], Galaxie, New Series, Oct 1966, No 30.

c. THE PRESERVING MACHINE, Ace 67800, 1969, paper.*

d. (as "Sindrome Regressiva") [Italian], I DIFENSORI DELLA TERRA, Fanucci: Futuro 34, 1977, paper.*

e. (as "Sindrome De Retirada") [Spanish], EN LA TIERRA SOMBRIA, Edhasa: 26, 1978, paper.*

f. (as "Syndrome De Retrait") [French], LES DÉLIRES DIVERGENTS DE PHILIP K. DICK, Ed by Alain Doremieux, Casterman, Paris, 1979.*

103.a. — interior.

104.a.

104. **"Return Match"** (4500 words)

Alien racketeers trap a vice-squad cop by using a living pin-ball machine as an instrument of vengeance.

"The theme of dangerous toys runs like a tattered thread throughout my writing. The dangerous disgused as the innocent . . . and what could be more innocent than a toy? This story makes me think of a set of huge speakers I looked at last week; they cost six thousand dollars and were larger than refrigerators. Our joke about them was that if you didn't go to the audio store to see them, they'd come to see **you.***"* — PKD

   a. Galaxy, Feb 1967.*
      Not illustrated.

   b. (as "Match Retour") [French], Galaxie, New Series, Oct 1967, No 42.

   c. (as "Match Retour") [French], LES DÉLIRES DIVERGENTS DE PHILIP K. DICK, Ed by Alain Doremieux, Casterman, Paris, 1979.*

   d. THE GOLDEN MAN, Ed by Mark Hurst, Berkley: 04288, 1980, paper.*

105. **"Roog"** (2050 words)

Author's first sold story.

A dog's-eye view of an inimical collection process.

"My first sale! And to Tony Boucher at F & SF. He made me work this story over to its very bones before he accepted it. But ah, that day a letter arrived in the mail, instead of a manuscript with a rejection slip! I love this story, and I doubt if I write any better today than I did in 1951, when I wrote it; I just write longer." — PKD

   a. Fantasy & Science Fiction, Feb 1953.*
      Not illustrated.

b. THE PRESERVING MACHINE, Ace: 67800, 1969, paper.*

c. THE OTHERS, Ed by Terry Carr, Fawcett: R2044 ($0.60), 1969, paper.*

d. INVADERS FROM SPACE, Ed by Robert Silverberg, Hawthorn, New York ($6.95), 1972.*

e. REFLECTIONS OF THE FUTURE, by Russell Hill, Ginn And Company, 1975, paper.
   Contains the story and an excerpt from an otherwise unpublished interview.

f. (as "Ruug") [Italian], LE VOCI DI DOPO, Fanucci: Futuro 26, 1976, paper.*

g. (as "Groem") [Dutch], DE ONMOGELIJKE PLANEET, A W Bruna: SF 40, 1976, paper.*

h. THE BEST OF PHILIP K. DICK, Ballantine: 25359, 1977, paper.*

i. (as "Rug") [Spanish], LA MAQUINA PRESERVADORA, Edhasa. 23, 1978, paper.*

j. (as "Reug") [French], LES DÉLIRES DIVERGENTS DE PHILIP K. DICK, Ed by Alain Doremieux, Casterman, Paris, 1979.*

k. Unearth, Winter 1979, Vol 2 No 4.*
   Quite substantial introduction added by the author.

106. "Sales Pitch" (9500 words)
Commuting distances have been raised by a power of 10^6, with a corresponding increase in advertising intensity.

"When this story first appeared, the fans detested it. I read it over, perplexed by their hostility, and could see why: it is a superdowner story, and relentlessly so. Could I rewrite it I would have it end differently, I would have the man and the robot, i.e. the fasrad, form a partnership at the end and become friends. The logic of paranoia of this story should be deconstructed into its opposite; Y, the human-against-robot theme, should have been resolved into null-Y, human-and-robot-against-the-universe. I really deplore the ending. So when you read the story, try to imagine it as it ought to have been written. The fasrad says, 'Sir, I am here to help you. The hell with my sales pitch. Let's be together forever.' Yes, but then I would have been criticized for a false upbeat ending, I guess. Still, this ending is not good. The fans were right."—PKD

a. Future, June 1954.*
   Illustrated by Luton.

b. (as "Vente A Outrance") [French], Satellite, Feb 1959, No 14.

c. THE GOLDEN MAN, Ed by Mark Hurst, Berkley: 04288, 1980, paper.*

107. "Schizophrenia & The Book Of Changes"
Non-Fiction.

PKD discusses the time-splitting qualities of LSD, schizophrenia, precognition and the Book of Changes.

a. Niekas, No 11, March 1965.

b. Cover, May 1974.

c. (as "Das Buch Der Wandlungen") [German], Science Fiction Times, Special Issue No 1: PHILIP K. DICK–MATERIALIEN, 1976.*

108. "Scientists Claim: We Are Center Of The Universe"
Non-Fiction.

a. New Worlds, No 216, Sept 1979.*

109. "Second Variety" (16000 words)
The automatic underground factories are in charge of prosecuting the war. Beyond human control, they begin to develop new weapons, the first of which are the claws which have taken total control of the surface.
"My grand theme—who is human and who only appears (masquerades) as human?—emerges most fully. Unless we can individually and collectively be certain of the answer to this question, we face what is, in my view, the most serious problem possible. Without answering it adequately, we cannot even be certain of our own selves. I cannot even know myself, let alone you. So I keep working on this theme; to me nothing is as important a question. And the answer comes very hard."—PKD

a. Space Science Fiction, May 1953.*
Illustrated by Ebel.

b. Space Science Fiction (British), Vol 1 No 5, May 1953.*

c. YEAR'S BEST SCIENCE FICTION NOVELS: 1954, Ed by E F Bleiler and T E Dikty, Frederick Fell, New York ($3.50), 1954.*
British editions omit the Dick story.

d. Selected Science Fiction Magazine (Australian), No 1, undated (May 1955).

e. THE VARIABLE MAN, Ace: D-261, 1957, paper.*

f. SPECTRUM II, Ed by Kingsley Amis and Robert Conquest, Gollancz, London (18/-), 1962.

g. (as "Modello Due") [Italian], Urania No 359, 1964.

h. (as "Type Twee") [Dutch], EEN HANDVOL DUISTERNIS, A W Bruna: 1100, 1968, paper.*

i. (as "Modello Due") [Italian], IL PASSO DELL'IGNOTO, Mondadori, Milan, 1972.
Translator: B della Frattina.

j. THE BEST SCIENCE-FICTION STORIES, Ed by Michael Stapleton, Hamlyn, London (£2.95), 1977.*

k. THE BEST OF PHILIP K. DICK, Ballantine: 25359, 1977, paper.*

l. (as "Modello Due") [Italian], L'UOMO VARIABILE, Fanucci: Futuro 45, 1979, paper.*
Translators: M Nati and T Tagliamonte.

110. "Service Call" (7600 words)

A repairman comes to adjust the Courtland's swibble. The only problem is that the Courtlands do not even have a swibble, because swibbles have not yet been invented.

"When this story appeared many fans objected to it because of the negative attitude I expressed in it. But I was already beginning to suppose in my head the growing domination of machines over man, especially the machines we voluntarily surround ourselves with, which should, by logic, be the most harmless. I never assumed that some huge clanking monster would stride down Fifth Avenue, devouring New York; I always feared that my own TV set or iron or toaster would, in the privacy of my apartment, when no one else was around to help, announce to me that it had taken over, and here was a list of rules I was to obey. I never like the idea of doing what a machine says. I hate having to salute something built in a factory. (Do you suppose all those White House tapes came out of the back of the President's head? And programmed him as to what he was to say and do?)"—PKD

    a. Science Fiction Stories, July 1955.*
       Illustrated by Kelly Freas.

    b. (as "Service De Reparation") [French], Satellite, Jan-Feb 1962, No 41.

    c. MASTERS OF SCIENCE FICTION, Anonymous, Belmont: 92-606 ($0.50), 1964, paper.*

    d. (as "Een Swibble Voor Dag En Nacht") [Dutch], EEN SWIBBLE VOOR DAG EN NACHT, A W Bruna: 1295, 1969, paper.*

    e. (as "Un' Occhiata Allo Svibblo") [Italian], Galassia No 210, 1975. Translator: V Curtoni.

    f. THE BEST OF PHILIP K. DICK, Ballantine: 25359, 1977, paper.*

111. "Shell Game" (5600 words)

Shipwrecked on Betelgeuse IV, a group of besieged survivors offer proof of the theory that it is not paranoid agression if you are really after someone.

    a. Galaxy, Sept 1954.*
       Illustrated by Kossin.

    b. (as "Rivolta Contro La Terra") [Italian], Galaxy, No 23, 1960.

    c. THE BOOK OF PHILIP K. DICK, DAW: 44, 1973, paper.*

    d. (as "Rivolta Contro La Terra") [Italian], I DIFENSORI DELLA TERRA, Fanucci: Futuro 34, 1977, paper.*

    e. (as "Dans La Coque") [French], LE LIVRE D'OR DE LA SCIENCE-FICTION: PHILIP K. DICK, Ed by Marcel Thaon, Presses Pocket: 5051, 1979, paper.*

112. "The Short Happy Life Of A Science Fiction Writer"
Non-Fiction.

    a. Scintillation, June 1976, Vol 3 No 3.*

113. **"The Short Happy Life Of The Brown Oxford"** (4400 words)

Doctor Rupert Labyrinth's Animator uses the principle of sufficient irritation to bring life to a family of shoes.

   a. Fantasy & Science Fiction, Jan 1954.*
      Not illustrated.

   b. Fantasy & Science Fiction (British), Vol 3 No 1, No 9, June 1954.*

   c. (as "Le Soulier Qui Trouva Chassure A Son Pied") [French], Fiction, Aug 1954, No 9.*

114. **"The Skull"** (8200 words)

Conger, a three-time loser, is given a chance to redeem himself. He is sent back in time to assassinate a mysterious religious leader whose only traces are a skull and one appearance in a small town.

   a. If, Sept 1952.*
      Not illustrated.

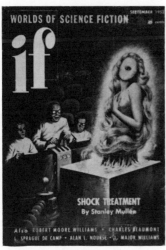

114.a.

116.a.

115. **"Small Town"** (5400 words)

An exercise in sympathetic magic by a frustrated model railroad builder.

"Here the frustrations of a defeated small person—small in terms of power, in particular power over others—gradually becomes transformed into something sinister: the force of death. In rereading this story (which is of course a fantasy, not science fiction) I am impressed by the subtle change which takes place in the protagonist from Trod-Upon to Treader. Verne Haskel initially appears as the prototype of the impotent human being, but this conceals a drive at his core self which is anything but weak. It is as if I am saying, The put-upon person may be very dangerous. Be careful as to how you misuse him; he may be a mask for thanatos: the antagonist of life; he may not secretly wish to rule; he may wish to **destroy.***"—PKD*

   a. Amazing, May 1954.*
      Illustrated by B Krigstein.

   b. Amazing (British), Third Series, Vol 1 No 5, undated (Aug 1954).

   c. Amazing, April 1967.*

   d. (as "Kleinsteeds") [Dutch], EEN SWIBBEL VOOR DAG EN NACHT, A W Bruna: 1295, 1969, paper.*

   e. (as "Le Petite Ville") [French], LE LIVRE D'OR DE LA SCIENCE-FICTION: PHILIP K. DICK, Ed by Marcel Thaon, Presses Pocket: 5051, 1979, paper.*

116.   "Some Kinds Of Life" (3500 words)
   As by Richard Phillipps.
   A society of super-colonialists destroys itself to maintain its gadgets.

   a. Fantastic Universe, Oct Nov 1953.*

117.   "Souvenir" (5300 words)
   Earth's first colony has been rediscovered—an atavism. Elsewhere, conformity has eliminated war. There can be no differences allowed to stimulate conflict, so the atavism must be destroyed.

   a. Fantastic Universe, Oct 1954.*
      Not illustrated.

118.   "Stand-By" (6000 words)
   Unicephalon 40-D is the mechanical supreme leader of the United States. Max Fischer is its human back-up; a union feather-bedder who succeeds to power when the computer is disabled.

   a. Amazing, Oct 1963.*
      Illustrated by Schelling.

   b. (as "Top Stand-By Job") THE PRESERVING MACHINE, Ace 67800, 1969, paper.*

   c. (as "Presidente Di Riserva") [Italian], LE VOCI DI DOPO, Fanucci: Futuro 26, 1976, paper.*

   d. (as "Top Stand-By Job") INSIDE INFORMATION, Ed by Abbe Mowshowitz, Addison-Wesley, Reading, 1977. (Hardcover ?)

   e. (as "Cargo De Suplente Maximo") [Spanish], LA MAQUINA PRESERVADORA, Edhasa: 23, 1978, paper.*

   f. (as "Une Sinecure") [French], LE LIVRE D'OR DE LA SCIENCE-FICTION: PHILIP K. DICK, Ed by Marcel Thaon, Presses Pocket: 5051, 1979, paper.*

119.   "The Story To End All Stories For Harlan Ellison's Anthology Dangerous Visions" (116 words)
   Another God-is-dead story outline.

a.   Niekas, No 20, Fall 1968.*

b.   (as "Den Sidste Historie") [Danish], Superlove, No 25, Oct 1969.*
Translator: Jannick Storm.

120. **"Strange Eden"** (5000 words)
A boorish explorer meets a beautiful immortal who shows him that evolution does not always take the expected course.

a.   Imagination, Dec 1954.*
Illustrated by W E Terry (?).

121. **"A Surface Raid"** (8100 words)
The technos have mutated and evolved underground after the Atomic wars. On the surface, their brethren have fallen into barbarism, but are highly prized as slaves by the technos.

a.   Fantastic Universe, July 1955.*
Not illustrated.

122. **"Survey Team"** (5700 words)
Earth is despoiled by war. The underground survivors try to colonize Mars, but find their ancestors have already used Mars up.

a.   Fantastic Universe, May 1954.*
Not illustrated.

123. **"That Moon Plaque"**
Non-Fiction.
Short statement about the wording of the plaque placed on the Moon by Apollo 11. (Individual statements by 28 science fiction authors all under the same title.)

a.   MEN ON THE MOON, Ed by Donald A Wollheim, Ace: 52470 ($0.60), 1969, paper.*
This is the second edition of this title which was originally published in 1958. Only the second edition carries this cited Dick work.

124. **"Three Sci-Fi Authors View The Future"**
Non-Fiction.
Three separate articles, under one title, by Philip K Dick, Michael Crichton, and Kurt Vonnegut.

a.   Voice, Vol 55 No 14, 17 Jan 1974.*

125. **"Time Out Of Joint"** (67000 words)
First published as TIME OUT OF JOINT.
Ragel Gumm believes himself to be a drone, living with his in-laws and supporting himself by anticipating patterns in a supposedly random newspaper contest. When Ragel accidently breaks out of his carefully

constructed reality, he discovers he is neither where, when nor whom he believes himself to be. His idle newspaper game is, in fact, the only thing preserving Earth's military dictatorship from destruction in the Lunar-Terran conflict.

a. New Worlds (British), sr3, Dec 1959*, Jan 1960, Feb 1960*, No 89, 90, 91.
Abriged from the book TIME OUT OF JOINT.

b. (as "L'Uomo Dei Giochi A Premia") [Italian], MILLEMONDINVERNO 1975: TRE ROMANZI COMPLETI DI PHILIP K. DICK, Mondadori: Supplemento A Urania 684, 1975, paper.*

126. "Time Pawn" (23200 words)

Later expanded into DR. FUTURITY.

A doctor is pulled 700 years forward through time. His first view is that of a society which needs no medical skills, because anyone sick or injured instantly volunteers for euthanasia to further a universal eugenics scheme. He has been time-napped to resuscitate a man whose family wants him to become the sole ancestor of the human race.

a. Thrilling Wonder Stories, Summer 1954.*
Illustrated by Virgil Finlay.

130.a.

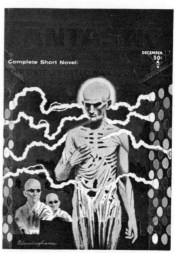

133.a.

127. "To Serve The Master" (4600 words)

The war is over—long over. The robots have been destroyed and their revolution quashed. But when Applequist finds one last damaged android moldering in a ditch he hears quite a different story.

a. Imagination, Feb 1956.*

128. "Tony And The Beetles" (4700 words)

Terrans took the Pas-Udeti system for their own. Tony played with the Pas-Udeti children as equals, but was the first to feel their hostile reaction when the Terran power began to ebb.

   a. Orbit Science Fiction, No 2, 1953.*
      Illustrator not credited.

   b. (as "Retreat From Rigel") PLANET OF DOOM AND OTHER STORIES (Australian), Jubilee Publications Pty Ltd, Sydney, undated (No 214, March 1958).
      This is the fourth issue of the "Satellite Series", whose numbering started with No 211.

"Top Stand-By Job"
    See "Stand-By"

129. "The Trouble With Bubbles" (6500 words)

Earth is isolated in the universe. Its frustrated inhabitants amuse themselves by forcing evolution in a series of miniscule world-bubbles. The tiny worlds are destroyed after an orgiastic exhibition. Trouble comes from two extremely frightening words: Direct Analogy.

   a. If, Sept 1953.*
      Illustrated by Joseph R Eberle.

   b. If (British), Vol 1 No 4, undated (Feb 1954).

   c. (as "Gli Imprudenti") [Italian], Oltre Il Cielo No 7, 1957.
      Translator: M Scotti.

130. "The Turning Wheel" (8400 words)

A stagnant society which believes in the transmigration of souls also believes in the futility of action. It attempts to educate the mechanically apt peasants, but one of its members is introduced to the radical doctrine of self-interest.

   a. Science Fiction Stories, No 2, 1954.*

   b. A HANDFUL OF DARKNESS, Rich & Cowan, London, 1955.*

   c. (as "La Roue Tourne") [French], Satellite, Sept 1961, No 37.

   d. NOW & BEYOND, Anonymous, Belmont: B50-646 ($0.50), 1965, paper.*

   e. THE BOOK OF PHILIP K. DICK, DAW: 44, 1973, paper.*

   f. (as "La Ruota Cosmica") [Italian], I DIFENSORI DELLA TERRA, Fanucci: Futuro 34, 1977, paper.*

131. "Universe Makers . . . And Breakers"
    Non-Fiction.

   a. SelecTV Guide, 15 Feb - 28 March, 1981.*

132. "The Unreconstructed M" (15600 words)

A germinal novel of genteel slavers, trans-galactic banishment for crimes and a homicidal homeostatic machine.

*"If the main theme throughout my writing is, 'Can we consider the universe real, and if so, in what way?' my secondary theme would be, 'Are we all humans?' Here a machine does not imitate a human being, but instead fakes evidence **of** a human being, a given human being. Fakery is a topic which absolutely fascinates me; I am convinced that anything can be faked, or anyhow evidence pointing to any given thing. Spurious clues can lead us to believe anything **they** want us to believe. There is really no theoretical upper limit to this. Once you have mentally opened the door to the reception of the notion of **fake**, you are ready to think yourself into another kind of reality entirely. It's a trip from which you never return. And, I think, a healthy trip . . . unless you take it too seriously."—PKD*

a. Science Fiction Stories, Jan 1957.
   Illustrated by Kelly Freas.

b. (as "La Machine À Detruire") [French], Satellite, Jan 1959, No 13.

c. THE GOLDEN MAN, Ed by Mark Hurst, Berkley: 04288, 1980, paper.*

133. "The Unteleported Man" (32000 words)

Of the Sol system's two mega-corporations, one has already been gutted and the other is still trying to stave off the German-run, fascistic United Nations government. The government is using a mysterious one-way teleportation system to populate a second Earth, but messages from this colony have been proven to be fakes. Rachmael von Applebaum wants to use the only remaining asset of his bankrupt corporation, an interstellar ship, to make the eighteen year physical journey to investigate the fate of millions of colonists.

a. Fantastic, Dec 1964.*
   Cover art for "The Unteleported Man" by Lloyd Birmingham. Interior illustrations by Schelling.

b. A PHILIP K. DICK OMNIBUS, Sidgwick & Jackson, London, 1970.*

c. SCIENCE FICTION SPECIAL 7, Anonymous, Sidgwick & Jackson, London, 1973 (?).

134. Untitled

Short non-fiction article in the section entitled "Limbo" (in Danish).

a. Victor B. Andersen's Maskinfabrik, No 4, 1976.*

135. Untitled

Unpublished foreword to THE PRESERVING MACHINE.

a. Science-Fiction Studies, No 5, Vol 2 Part 1, March 1975.*

136. "Upon The Dull Earth" (8300 words)

Sylvia's mystical attraction for angel-like beings from another continuum results in her premature transcendance. On her return, we find she has become rather common.

a. Beyond Fantasy Fiction, Nov 1954, No 9.*

b. A HANDFUL OF DARKNESS, Rich & Cowan, London, 1955.*

c. (as "En Ce Bas Mondo") [French], HISTOIRES DES TEMPS FUTURE, Ed by Alain Doremieux, Casterman, Paris, 1968.*

d. (as "De Saaie Aarde") [Dutch], EEN HANDVOL DUISTERNIS, A W Bruna: 1100, 1968, paper.*

e. THE PRESERVING MACHINE, Ace: 67800, 1969, paper.*

f. (as "Sulla Nera Terra") [Italian], LE VOCI DI DOPO, Fanucci: Futuro 26, 1976, paper.*

g. (as "En La Tierra Sombria") [Spanish], EN LA TIERRA SOMBRIA, Edhasa 26, 1978, paper.*

137. **"The Variable Man"** (2600 words)

Earth is at a disadvantage in the Proximan war. The computer puts the odds against Earth because of its failure to develop its FTL weapon. Cole, a man accidentally dredged from the past, is the only master technician who could finish the weapon. He becomes the object of a deadly manhunt because his presence presents the computer with an incalculable variable.

a. Space Science Fiction (British), Vol 2 No 2, July 1953.*

b. Space Science Fiction, Sept 1953.*
Illustrated by Ebel.

c. THE VARIABLE MAN, Ace: D-261, 1957, paper.*

d. (as "L'Uomo Variabile") [Italian], L'UOMO VARIABILE, Fanucci: Futuro 45, 1979, paper.*

137.b. — interior.

138. "Vulcan's Hammer" (22800 words)

After the Atomic war, men turn over control of their society to Vulcan III, a computer. In the static civilization thus created, forces from the lower strata led by the Healers threaten stability. There are also certain intimations that Vulcan III has come alive, that it is not the impartial controller it once was, and that it will fight for its survival.

a. Future, No 29, 1956.*
Cover art for "Vulcan's Hammer" and story illustration by Kelly Freas.

b. (as "Le Marteu De Vulcain") [French], Satellite, Aug 1959, No 20.

c. 6 AND THE SILENT SCREAM, Ed by Ivan Howard, Belmont: L92-564 ($0.50), 1963, paper.*

d. (as "El Martillo De Vulcano") [Spanish], ANTOLOGIA DE NOVELAS DE ANTICIPACION–VOLUMEN TERCERO, Ediciones Acervo, Barcelona, 1975 (?).

139. "War Game" (5700 words)

The Ganymedeans are engaged in a long-range economic war with the inner planets.

a. Galaxy, Dec 1959.*
Illustrated by Wood.

b. (as "Il Gioco Della Guerra") [Italian], Galaxy, No 34, 1961.

c. (as "Jeu De Guerre") [French], Galaxie, New Series, May 1965, No 13.

d. THE PRESERVING MACHINE, Ace: 67800, 1969, paper.*

e. (as "Il Gioco Della Guerra") [Italian], LE VOCI DI DOPO, Fanucci: Futuro 26, 1976, paper.*

f. (as "Juego De Guerra") [Spanish], LA MAQUINA PRESERVADORA, Edhasa: 23, 1978, paper.*

g. (as "Jeu De Guerre") [French], LES DÉLIRES DIVERGENTS DE PHILIP K. DICK, Ed by Alain Doremieux, Casterman, Paris, 1979.*

h. THE 13 CRIMES OF SCIENCE FICTION, Ed by Isaac Asimov, Martin Harry Greenberg and Charles G Waugh, Doubleday, Garden City ($12.50), 1979.*

140. "War Veteran" (16900 words)

The Sol system is about to explode into an internecine conflict: Terrans against the Venusian "webfeet" and Martian "crows." An old man, Donald Unger, appears as a time-jumper. He is a veteran of the war that has not yet been fought, bringing the news to Earth that it cannot win the upcoming war.

a. If, March 1955.*
   Illustrated by Kelly Freas.

b. (as "L'Ancien Combattant") [French], Univers, No 10, 1955 (?).

c. THE PRESERVING MACHINE, Ace: 67800, 1969, paper.*

d. (as "De Oorlogs Veteraan") [Dutch], DE ONMOGELIJKE PLANEET, A W
   Bruna: SF 40, 1976, paper.*

e. (as "Veterano Di Guerra") [Italian], LI VOCI DI DOPO, Fanucci: Futuro
   26, 1976, paper.*

f. (as "Veterano De Guerra") [Spanish], LA MAQUINA PRESERVADORA,
   Edhasa: 23, 1978, paper.*

141. "The War With The Fnools"

**As 60-centimeter tall real-estate salesmen, the inimical Fnools are
relatively easy to detect and defeat. Then the Fnools are introduced to
the three bad kings.**

*"Well, once again we are invaded. And, humiliatingly, by a life form which
is absurd. My colleague Tim Powers once said that Martians could invade
us simply by putting on funny hats, and we'd never notice. It's a sort of low-
budget invasion. I guess we're at the point where we can be amused by the
idea of Earth being invaded. (And this is when they really zap you.)"*—PKD

a. Galaxy, Feb 1969.*
   Illustated by Jones.

b. (as "Bacco, Tabacco E . . . Fnools") [Italian], Urania No 520, 1969.

c. (as "Il Punto Debole Degli Sfnul") [Italian], QUESTA NOTTE ATTENTI
   AGLI UFO, Ed by Carlo Fruttero and Franco Lucentini, Mondadori,
   1978.*
   Translator: Mario Galli.

d. THE GOLDEN MAN, Ed by Mark Hurst, Berkley: 04288, 1980, paper.*

142. "Waterspider" (12100 words)

**Twenty-first century scientists turn to the great pre-cogs of the Twen-
tieth century for the answers to their space flight problems. Among the
pre-cogs are A.E. Van Vogt, Murray Leinster and Jack Vance. In fact,
the time dredge brings up Poul Anderson for a vital consultation.**

a. If, Jan 1964.*
   Illustrated by Virgil Finlay.

b. (as "Pulce D'Acqua") [Italian], Urania No 336, 1964.
   Translator: B della Frattina.

c. (as "Project Argyronete") [French], Galaxie, New Series, Nov 1965, No
   19.

143. "We Can Remember It For You Wholesale"

Douglas Quail has several obsessions: he wants to go to Mars and he wants to save the Earth. At the artificial memory emporium, he realizes that he has already been to Mars. . . .

a. Fantasy & Science Fiction, April 1966.*
Not illustrated.

b. (as "De Memoire D'Homme") [French], Fiction, Aug 1966, No 153.

c. THE BEST FROM FANTASY AND SCIENCE FICTION 16TH SERIES, Ed by Edward L Ferman, Doubleday, Garden City ($4.50), 1967.*

d. NEBULA AWARD STORIES II, Ed by Brian W Aldiss and Harry Harrison, Gollancz, London (25/-), 1967.*
Released in the U.S. as NEBULA AWARD STORIES TWO.

e. WORLD'S BEST SCIENCE FICTION: 1967, Ed by Donald A Wollheim and Terry Carr, Ace: A-10 ($0.75), 1967, paper.*

f. (as "Chi Se Lo Ricorda?") [Italian], Urania No 490, 1968.
Translator: B della Frattina.

g. THE PRESERVING MACHINE, Ace: 67800, 1969, paper.*

h. (as "Ricordo Per Tutti") [Italian], Italsider No 20, 1969, paper.*

i. (as "Herinneringen En Gros") [Dutch], SCIENCE FICTION-VERHALEN, Het Spectrum, 1969, paper (?).

j. TWENTY YEARS OF FANTASY & SCIENCE FICTION, Ed by Edward L Ferman and Robert P Mills, Putnam, New York ($5.95), 1970.*

k. (as   ) [Urdu], 1971.
Translated by the United States Information Agency for publication in Pakistan. However no further information is available as to the actual title or exactly where published.

l. (as "Podemos Lembra-lo Para Voce Por Atacado") [Portuguese], Magazine de Ficcao Cientifica, No 16, July 1971.*
Translator: Rosaura Eichenberg. Published in Brazil.

m. (as   ) [Hungarian], Tancsics (Publisher), 1974.

n. ALPHA 5, Ed by Robert Silverberg, Ballantine: 24140 ($1.25), 1974, paper.*

o. EARTH IN TRANSIT, Ed by Sheila Schwartz, Dell: 2262 ($1.25), 1976, paper.

p. (as "Ricordi In Vendita") [Italian], I DIFENSORI DELLA TERRA, Fanucci: Futuro 34, 1977, paper.*

q. THE MAGAZINE OF FANTASY & SCIENCE FICTION: A 30 YEAR RETROSPECTIVE, Ed by Edward L Ferman, Doubleday, Garden City ($10.00), 1980.

144. "What The Dead Men Say" (17000 words)

Manuscript title "Man With A Broken Match".

An election plot is masterminded by Kathy Sharp, a monstrous psychotic operating in the guise of Louis Serapis, the most powerful corpse in the Solar System. In this story, Dick accurately predicted Nixon's political comeback, then four years in the future.

    a. Worlds of Tomorrow, June 1964.*
         Illustrated by Virgil Finlay.

    b. (as "La Voix Venue Du Ciel") [French], Galaxie, New Series, Oct 1964, No 6.

    c. THE PRESERVING MACHINE, Ace: 67800, 1969, paper.*

    d. (as "Le Voci Di Dopo") [Italian], LE VOCI DI DOPO, Fanucci: Futuro 26, 1976, paper.*

    e. (as "Lo Que Dicen Los Muertos") [Spanish], EN LA TIERRA SOMBRIA, Edhasa: 26, 1978, paper.*

    f. (as "Ce Que Disent Les Morts") [French], LES DÉLIRES DIVERGENTS DE PHILIP K. DICK, Ed by Alain Doremieux, Casterman, Paris, 1979.*

145. "What'll We Do With Ragland Park?" (6000 words)

Manuscript title "No Ordinary Guy".

The venal head of a television network discovers a folk-singer whose ballads have a cause and effect relationship with reality.

    a. Amazing, Nov 1963.*
         Illustrated by Virgil Finlay.

    b. The Most Thrilling Science Fiction Ever Told, Summer 1969, No 13.

146. "Who Is A SF Writer?"

Non-Fiction.

    a. SCIENCE FICTION: THE ACADEMIC AWAKENING, Ed by Willis E McNelly, College English Association, 1974, paper.*

147. "Why I Am Hurt"

Verse.

A short poem, about 12 lines as Dick remembers.

    a. A CHILD'S HAT, Ed by Ward J Gulyas, Published by the editor, 1966, paper.

148. "Will The Atomic Bomb Ever Be Perfected, And If So, What Becomes Of Robert Heinlein"

Non-Fiction.

A group of anecdotal one-liners concerning the world (and craft) of Science Fiction.

    a. Lighthouse, No 14, Oct 1966.*

149.   "The World Jones Made"

First published as THE WORLD JONES MADE.

Fed-gov is reconstructing the post-war world according to the precepts of relativism. Jones, a former carnival fortune-teller and preacher who can see a year into the future, says the alien drifters, origin unknown, are the greatest threat the world faces; a problem the Fed-gov refuses to address. Jones forms a fanatical organization to deal with the drifters and the Fed-gov.

    a. SCIENCE FICTION SPECIAL 1, Anonymous, Sidgwick & Jackson, London, 1970.

150.   "A World Of Talent" (14400 words)

The Psis have revolted against Earth to save their own lives, but they have a bigger problem. Psis stretch the checks and balances of the world line. They must learn to control their own powers.

    a. Galaxy, Oct 1954.*
       Illustrated by Kossin.

    b. (as "Eine Welt Der Talente") [German], Galaxis, No 15, undated, 1955 (?)*

    c. THE VARIABLE MAN, Ace: D-261, 1957, paper.*

    d. (as "Un Monde De Talents") [French], HISTOIRES DE MUTANTS, Ed by Gerard Klein, Le Livre de Poche: 3766, 1974, paper.*

    e. (as "Un Mondo Di Geni") [Italian], L'UOMO VARIABILE, Fanucci: Futuro 45, 1979, paper.*

142.a.

151.a.

151. **"The World She Wanted"** (6700 words)

   Allison Holmes owns a world in a sheaf of alternate continuums of which she is the absolute, probability-defying mistress. She wants Larry Brewster to share it with her.

   a. Science Fiction Quarterly, May 1953.*
   Cover and interior art for "The World She Wanted" by Milton Luros.

   b. Science Fiction Quarterly (British), No 6, undated (May 1954).*

152. **"Your Appointment Will Be Yesterday"**

   Expanded as COUNTER-CLOCK WORLD.

   The Hobart Phase reverses entropy: bodies coalesce in the grave, food is regurgitated and phone conversations begin with: "Goodbye." The problem is, the uninvention of the swabble must be stopped.

   a. Amazing, Aug 1966.*
   Illustrated by Gray Morrow.

   b. (as "Rendez-Vous Hier Matin") [French], LE LIVRE D'OR DE LA SCIENCE-FICTION: PHILIP K. DICK, Ed by Marcel Thaon, Presses Pocket: 5051, 1979, paper.*

UNPUBLISHED MANUSCRIPTS

There is a collection of Phil Dick's manuscripts in the Special Collection Section of the California State University, Fullerton. For a full description of the collection, both published and unpublished material, see Science-Fiction Studies, No 5, Vol 2 Part 1, March 1975.

The story "No Ordinary Guy", listed as unpublished in the above article, is actually the published story "What'll We Do With Ragland Park?". Also, Phil Dick states that the story "Sir Waldo And Sir Lunchalot", which is included in the collection, is not by him but by another author (whose name he does not remember) and was accidentally included in the manuscript collection. Ignoring fragments and other miscellaneous works, the remaining unpublished manuscripts are:

NOVELS

General Fiction:
The Broken Bubble Of Thisbe Holt (350 pages)
Gather Yourselves Together (481 pages)
In Milton Lumky Territory (293 pages)
The Man Whose Teeth Were All Exactly Alike (358 pages)
Mary And The Giant (315 pages)
Puttering About In A Small Land (416 pages)
Voices From The Street (652 pages)

Science Fiction:
The Unteleported Man (second half)

SHORT WORKS

Fiction:
Joe Protagoras Is Alive And Living On Earth (TV Outline)
Orpheus With Clay Feet (4000 words)
Warning: We Are Your Police (TV Outline, 4800 words)

Non-Fiction:
A Good Savoyard Is A Dead Savoyard (14 pages—article on Gilbert and Sullivan)
How To Build A Universe That Doesn't Fall Apart Two Days Later (32 pages—
    Speech. Not in the Fullerton collection)

OTHER MEDIA

A number of Philip K Dick's works have been adapted for radio, TV and the screen. None of the adaptations was done by Dick.

Radio:

"Colony"—aired on "X Minus One" 10 Oct 1956.

"The Defenders"—aired on "X Minus One" 22 May 1956.

TV:

"The Cookie Lady"—half hour show aired by Metromedia sometime in the 1970s.

MARTIAN TIME SLIP—extensive effort aired on the BBC sometime in the 1960s.

Screen:

DO ANDROIDS DREAM OF ELECTRIC SHEEP?—Filming finished in mid 1981, having been budgeted at 20 million dollars from TAT/Tandem: screenplay by Hampton Fancher; director: Ridley Scott; producer: Michael Deeley. The film is titled BLADE RUNNER and stars Harrison Ford as the police bounty hunter Rick Decard.

"Second Variety"—Screen rights purchased by Capitol pictures; producer: Daniel Gilbertson; director: Daniel O'Bannon; screenplay: Daniel O'Bannon. The screenplay is completed.

UBIK—a screenplay was bought by French producer Jean-Pierre Gorin but the option has run out so it appears that it will not be filmed.

"We Can Remember It For You Wholesale"—A screenplay has been written by Daniel O'Bannon. The film is to be titled TOTAL RECALL. The filming is being financed by Disney Studios and filming is expected to begin in early 1982.

Philip K Dick also wrote three radio scripts which were aired in the mid-fifties on a show narrated by John W Campbell Jr on the Mutual Broadcasting System. Although Dick taped the shows he no longer has the tapes or any record of the exact dates of airing.

PSEUDONYMS

Richard Phillipps
 "Some Kinds Of Life"

Philip K Dick also published 16 pieces, including four poems, while he was in junior high school. These were published in Aunt Flo's "Young Author's Club" column in the Berkeley Daily Gazette in 1942-43. They were written under the names Phil Dick, Philip K. Dick and two as Mark van Dyke.

COLLABORATIONS

Ray Nelson
 THE GANYMEDE TAKEOVER

Roger Zelazny
 DEUS IRAE

CONNECTED STORIES AND CONTINUING CHARACTERS

CONTINUING CHARACTERS

Jim Briskin
"Cantata 140" (THE CRACK IN SPACE)
"The Mold Of Yancy"
"Stand-By" ("Top Stand-By Job")
THE THREE STIGMATA OF PALMER ELDRITCH
"What'll We Do With Ragland Park?"

Pat Conley
"A World Of Talent"
UBIK

Doc Labyrinth
"The Preserving Machine"
"The Short Happy Life Of The Brown Oxford"

Wilbur Mercer
"The Little Black Box"
DO ANDROIDS DREAM OF ELECTRIC SHEEP?

Herbert Schoenheit von Vogelsang
"What The Dead Men Say"
UBIK

CONNECTED STORIES

"Cantata 140" (THE CRACK IN SPACE)
"Prominent Author"

"The Days Of Perky Pat"
THE THREE STIGMATA OF PALMER ELDRITCH

"The Defenders"
"The Mold Of Yancy"
THE PENULTIMATE TRUTH

"The Great C"
"A Planet For Transients"
DEUS IRAE

"Jon's World"
"Second Variety"

"Novelty Act"
THE SIMULACRA

VALIS
"Chains Of Air, Web Of Aether"
THE DIVINE INVASION
BISHOP TIMOTHY ARCHER

"Your Appointment Will Be Yesterday"
COUNTER-CLOCK WORLD

NON-FICTION INDEX

VERSE INDEX

CHRONOLOGICAL ORDER OF PUBLICATION
OF PHILIP K DICK'S WORK

1952

"Beyond Lies The Wub"
"The Gun"
"The Skull"
"The Little Movement"

1953

"The Defenders"
"Mr. Spaceship"
"Piper In The Woods"
"Roog"
"The Infinites"
"Second Variety"
"The World She Wanted"
"Colony"
"The Cookie Lady"
"Impostor"
"Martians Come In Clouds"
"Paycheck"
"The Preserving Machine"
"The Cosmic Poachers"
"Expendable"
"The Indefatigable Frog"
"The Commuter"
"Out In The Garden"
"The Great C"
"The King Of The Elves"
"The Trouble With Bubbles"
"The Variable Man"
"The Impossible Planet"
"Planet For Transients"
"Some Kinds Of Life"
"The Builder"
"The Hanging Stranger"
"Project: Earth"
"The Eyes Have It"
"Tony And The Beetles"

1954

"Prize Ship"
"Beyond The Door"
"The Crystal Crypt"
"A Present For Pat"

"The Short Happy Life Of
The Brown Oxford"
"The Golden Man"
"James P. Crow"
"Prominent Author"
"Small Town"
"Survey Team"
"Sales Pitch"
"Time Pawn"
"Breakfast At Twilight"
"The Crawlers"
"Of Withered Apples"
"Exhibit Piece"
"Adjustment Team"
"Shell Game"
"Meddler"
"Souvenir"
"A World Of Talent"
"The Last Of The Masters"
"Progeny"
"Upon The Dull Earth"
"The Father-Thing"
"Strange Eden"
"Jon's World"
"The Turning Wheel"

1955

"Foster, You're Dead"
"Human Is"
"War Veteran"
"Captive Market"
"Nanny"
"The Hood Maker"
"The Chromium Fence"
"Service Call"
"A Surface Raid"
"The Mold Of Yancy"
"Autofac"
"Psi-Man Heal My Child!"
A HANDFUL OF DARKNESS
(Collection)
SOLAR LOTTERY

1956
"The Minority Report"
"To Serve The Master"
"Pay For The Printer"
"A Glass Of Darkness"
"Vulcan's Hammer"
THE WORLD JONES MADE
THE MAN WHO JAPED

1957
"The Unreconstructed M"
"Misadjustment"
EYE IN THE SKY
THE COSMIC PUPPETS
THE VARIABLE MAN (Collection)

1958
"Null-0"

1959
"Explorers We"
"Recall Mechanism"
"Fair Game"
"War Game"
TIME OUT OF JOINT

1960
DR. FUTURITY
VULCAN'S HAMMER

1961

1962
THE MAN IN THE HIGH CASTLE

1963
"All We Marsmen"
"Stand-By"
"What'll We Do With Ragland Park?"
"The Days Of Perky Pat"
"If There Were No Benny Cemoli"
THE GAME-PLAYERS OF TITAN

1964
"Waterspider"
"Novelty Act"

"Oh, To Be A Blobel!"
"What The Dead Men Say"
"Cantata 140"
"A Game Of Unchance"
"The Little Black Box"
"Naziism And The High Castle"
"Precious Artifact"
"Drugs, Hallucinations, And The
   Quest For Reality"
"The Unteleported Man"
THE PENULTIMATE TRUTH
MARTIAN TIME-SLIP
THE SIMULACRA
CLANS OF THE ALPHANE MOON

1965
"Retreat Syndrome"
"Schizophrenia & The Book Of
   Changes"
"Project Plowshare"
THE THREE STIGMATA OF
   PALMER ELDRITCH
DR. BLOODMONEY, OR HOW WE
   GOT ALONG AFTER THE BOMB

1966
"We Can Remember It For You
   Wholesale"
"Holy Quarrel"
"Your Appointment Will Be
   Yesterday"
"The Above And Melting"
"An Old Snare"
"Why I Am Hurt"
"Will The Atomic Bomb Ever Be
   Perfected, And If So, What
   Becomes Of Robert Heinlein?"
NOW WAIT FOR LAST YEAR
THE CRACK IN SPACE
THE UNTELEPORTED MAN

1967
"Return Match"
"Faith Of Our Fathers"
THE ZAP GUN
COUNTER-CLOCK WORLD

GANYMEDE TAKEOVER

1968
"Not By Its Cover"
"Anthony Boucher"
"The Story To End All Stories For
    Harlan Ellison's Anthology
    Dangerous Visions"
DO ANDROIDS DREAM OF
    ELECTRIC SHEEP?

1969
"The War With The Fnools"
"The Electric Ant"
"A. Lincoln, Simulacrum"
"That Moon Plaque"
GALACTIC POT-HEALER
UBIK
THE PRESERVING MACHINE
    (Collection)
EEN SWIBBEL VOOR DAG EN NACHT
    (Dutch Collection)

1970
A MAZE OF DEATH
OUR FRIENDS FROM FROLIX 8
A PHILIP K. DICK OMNIBUS
    (Collection)

1971

1972
"Notes Made Late At Night By A
    Weary SF Writer"
"The Android And The Human"
WE CAN BUILD YOU

1973
"The Nixon Crowd"
THE BOOK OF PHILIP K. DICK
    (Collection)

1974
"Three Sci-Fi Authors View The
    Future"
"The Pre-Persons"

"An Open Letter To Joanna Russ"
"A Little Something For Us
    Tempunauts"
"Who Is A SF Writer?"
FLOW MY TEARS, THE POLICEMAN
    SAID

1975
Untitled—Unpublished foreward to
    THE PRESERVING MACHINE
"The Evolution Of A Vital Love"
CONFESSIONS OF A CRAP ARTIST
MILLEMONDINVERNO 1975: TRE
    ROMANZI COMPLETI DI PHILIP
    K. DICK (Italian Collection)
LE RETOUR DES EXPLORATEURS
    (French)

1976
"Memories Found In A Bill From
    A Small Animal Vet"
"The Short Happy Life Of A
    Science Fiction Writer"
Untitled—Short aritcle in Danish
    (see STORIES No 134)
"Man, Android And Machine"
DEUS IRAE
DE ONMOGELIJKE PLANEET
    (Dutch Collection)

1977
THE BEST OF PHILIP K. DICK
    (Collection)
A SCANNER DARKLY

1978
"If You Find This World Bad, You
    Should See Some Of The
    Others" (in French)

1979
"The Exit Door Leads In"
"The Lucky Dog Pet Store"
"Scientists Claim: We Are Center
    Of The Universe"
LES DÉLIRES DIVERGENTS DE

PHILIP K. DICK (French Collection)
LE LIVRE D'OR DE LA SCIENCE-
  FICTION: PHILIP K. DICK
  (French Collection)

1980
"Chains Of Air, Web Of Aether"
"Rautavaara's Case"
"Frozen Journey"
THE GOLDEN MAN (Collection)

1981
"Universe Makers . . . And Breakers"
"The Alien Mind"
"His Predictions"
VALIS
THE DIVINE INVASION

FORTHCOMING
BISHOP TIMOTHY ARCHER
THE OWL IN DAYLIGHT

MAGAZINE CHECKLIST

Magazines which have material by Philip K Dick are listed in this section. "Magazine" is used somewhat loosely to include periodicals of all kinds but not quite loosely enough to include yearly compilations. Fanzines and semi-prozines are treated the same as professional magazines. Issues which contain only letters from Dick are not included. A number of the magazines do not actually have a date on them; however, where a date was available from some other source, it is given. The number in parentheses following each issue listing is the number of the work as given in the STORIES section of this bibliography.

Amazing
>Aug-Sept 1953 (18); Dec 1953 (12); May 1954 (115); July 1954 (11); Oct 1963 (118); Nov 1963 (145); Dec 1963 (24); July 1964 (41); Aug 1966 (152); Dec 1966 (18); April 1967 (115); June 1967 (12); Nov 1969 (1); Jan 1970 (1).

Amazing (British)—Third Series
>Vol 1 No 1, Dec 1953 (18); Vol 1 No 3, April 1954 (12); Vol 1 No 5, Aug 1954 (115); Vol 1 No 6, Oct 1954 (11).

The Aquarian
>11 Oct - 18 Oct 1978 (57-d).

Astounding
>June 1963 (54).

Astounding (British)
>Nov 1953 (54)

Beyond Fantasy Fiction
>Sept 1953 (60); Nov 1954, No 9 (136).

Cosmos Science Fiction And Fantasy
>Sept 1953, No 1 (44); July 1954, No 4 (82).

Cover
>May 1974 (107).

Eternity Science Fiction
>No 1, July 1972 (79).

Famous Science Fiction
>Summer 1968 (78).

Fantascienza (Italian)
>No 2, 1976 (87).

Fantastic
>Feb 1964 (80); Dec 1964 (133); Nov 1966 (11).

Fantastic Story Magazine
>July 1953 (55).

Fantastic Universe
>June-July 1953 (68); Oct-Nov 1953 (90, 116); Jan 1954 (10); May 1954 (122); Oct 1954 (117); July 1955 (121); Jan 1956 (71).

Fantasy & Science Fiction
>Nov 1952 (64); Feb 1953 (105); June 1953 (94); July 1953 (33); Jan 1954 (113); Dec 1954 (38); Jan 1959 (34); July 1964 (13); April 1966 (143); Aug 1968 (7); Oct 1969 (29); Oct 1974 (91).

Fantasy & Science Fiction (Australian)
>No 4, Aug 1955 (33).

Fantasy & Science Fiction (British)
>Vol 1 No 4, Jan 1954 (33); Vol 3 No 1, No 9, June 1954 (113).

Fantasy Fiction
>June 1953 (19); Aug 1953 (86).

Fiction (French)
>March 1954, No 4 (33); Aug 1954, No 9 (113); April 1956, No 29 (38); April 1965, No 137 (34); Aug 1966, No 153 (143); May 1967, No 162 (64); Feb 1969, No 182 (13); May 1969, No 185 (99); Aug 1969, No 188 (37), Jan 1970, No 193 (19); June 1970, No 198 (29); Aug 1972, No 224 (12); Oct 1972, No 226 (96).

Foundation (British)
>No 17, Sept 1979 (66).

Future
>June 1954 (106); Oct 1954 (69); No 29, 1956 (138).

Galassia (Italian)
>No 44, 1964 (51); No 210, 1975 (110).

Galaxie (French)
>Old Series: Sept 1954, No 10 (17); Aug 1956, No 33 (8).
>New Series: Aug 1964, No 4 (54); Sept 1964, No 5 (25); Oct 1964, No 6 (144); Nov 1964, No 7 (83); May 1965, No 13 (139); Nov 1965, No 19 (142); Feb 1966, No 22 (51); March 1966, No 23 (92); Oct 1966, No 30 (103); Dec 1966, No 32 (5); Jan 1967, No 33 (5); Feb 1967, No 34 (5); June 1967, No 38 (63); Nov 1967, No 43 (48); Oct 1967, No 42 (104); Nov 1968, No 54 (98); Dec 1968, No 55 (98).

Galaxis (German)
>No 5 (25); No 7 (17); No 15 (150).

Galaxy
>Jan 1953 (25); June 1953 (17); Sept 1954 (111); Oct 1954 (150); Nov 1955 (8); Dec 1959 (139); Dec 1963 (51); Feb 1964 (83); Oct 1964 (92); Feb 1967 (104); Feb 1969 (141).

Galaxy (British)
>Vol 3 No 5, June 1953 (25); Vol 3 No 8, Oct 1953 (17).

Galaxy (Italian)
>No 8, 1957 (8); No 23, 1960 (111); No 34, 1961 (139).

The Hartford Advocate
>22 April 1981 (57-i).

If
> Sept 1952 (114); Sept 1953 (129); April 1954 (43); May 1954 (99); Aug 1954 (31); Nov 1954 (96); March 1955 (140); April 1955 (14); Aug 1955 (73); Dec 1958 (81); July 1959 (102); Sept 1959 (36); Jan 1964 (142).

If (British)
> Vol 1 No 4, Feb 1954 (129); Vol 1 No 9, July 1954 (43); Vol 1 No 10, Aug 1954 (99); Vol 1 No 13, Nov 1954 (31).

Imagination
> Jan 1953 (74); Feb 1953 (89); June 1953 (88); July 1953 (20); Oct 1953 (53); Dec 1953 (97); July 1954 (22); Dec 1954 (120); June 1955 (49); July 1955 (16); Feb 1956 (127).

Imaginative Tales
> Nov 1955 (100).

Lighthouse
> No 11, Nov 1964 (28); No 14, Oct 1966 (148).

Magazine de Ficcao Cientifica (Brazilian)
> No 16, July 1971 (143).

Marginal (French)
> Nov-Dec 1973, No 1 (17); Sept-Oct 1974, No 5 (8).

Mike Bailey's Personalzine
> No 20, The Long Goodbye, May 1975 (30); The Long Hello (?), 1975 (?) (30).

The Most Thrilling Science Fiction Ever Told
> Summer 1968, No 9 (24); Summer 1969, No 13 (145).

New Worlds (British)
> No 89, Dec 1959 (125); No 90, Jan 1960 (125); No 91, Feb 1960 (125); No 216, Sept 1979 (108).

The New Yorker
> 27 Jan 1975 (57-b); 3 Feb 1975 (57-b).

Niekas
> No 9, 1964 (76); No 11, March 1965 (107); No 20, Fall 1968 (119).

Nouvelles Frontières (French)
> No 1, 1975 (91)

Nova SF (Italian)
> No 12, 1970 (94); No 13, 1971 (54); No 30, 1975 (89).

Nova 2001 (German)
> No 1/2, Jan-Feb 1979 (57-f).

Oltre Il Cielo (Italian)
> No 7, 1957 (129).

Ogonek (Russian)
> April 1958 (39).

Omni
Oct 1980 (101).

Opzone (French)
March 1980, No 7 (32).

Orbit Science Fiction
No 2, 1953 (128); Sept-Oct 1954, No 4 (3); Nov-Dec 1954, No 5 (61).

Planet Stories
July 1952 (9); Sept 1952 (45); May 1953 (56); Jan 1954 (23); May 1954 (58).

Playboy
Dec 1980 (40).

Point Final (Swiss)
No 3, 1979 (57-e).

Popular Science Fiction (Australian)
Vol 1 No 2, Nov 1953 (89).

Povestiri Stiintifico-Fantastice (Rumanian)
June 1958, No 82 (39).

The Real World
No 5, Feb-March 1976 (70).

Robot (Italian)
No 15, 1977 (65).

Rolling Stone College Papers
Fall 1979, No 1 (32).

SF Commentary (Australian)
No 31, Dec 1972 (6); No 39, Nov 1973 (77).

SF Greats
Fall 1970 (41).

SF Yearbook, A Treasury of Science Fiction
No 4, 1970 (93).

Satellite (French)
Dec 1958, No 12 (69); Jan 1959, No 13 (132); Feb 1959, No 14 (106); Aug 1959, No 20 (138); Sept 1961, No 37 (130); Jan-Feb 1962, No 41 (110).

Satellite Science Fiction
Oct 1956 (87); Dec 1956 (42).

Satellite Series (Australian)
SPACE STATION 42 AND OTHER STORIES, No 212, March 1958 (61); THE SANDS OF MARS AND OTHER STORIES, No 213, March 1958 (3); PLANET OF DOOM AND OTHER STORIES, No 214, March 1958 (128).

Science Fiction Adventures
Dec 1953 (46).

Science Fiction Monthly (Australian)
No 7, March 1956 (44); No 12, Aug 1956 (45); No 18, Feb 1957 (56).

Science Fiction Quarterly
May 1953 (151); Feb 1957 (72).

Science Fiction Quarterly (British)
No 6, May 1954 (151).

Science Fiction Review
No 19, Aug 1976 (57-c).

Science Fiction Stories
No 1, 1953 (35); No 2, 1954 (130); July 1955 (110); Jan 1957 (132).

Science-Fiction Studies
Vol 2 Part 1, No 5, March 1975 (135).

Science Fiction Times (German)
No 134, 1974 (77); Special Issue No 1: PHILIP K. DICK – MATERIALIEN, 1976
(6, 57-a, 77, 107); No 146, 1979 (57-g).

Scintillation
June 1976, Vol 3 No 3 (112)

Selected Science Fiction Magazine (Australian)
No 1, May 1955 (109).

SelecTV Guide
15 Feb - 28 March 1981 (131).

Space Science Fiction
May 1953 (109); Sept 1953 (137).

Space Science Fiction (British)
Vol 1 No 5, May 1953 (109); Vol 2 No 2, July 1953 (137).

Startling Stories
Jan 1954 (93); Winter 1955 (50); Spring 1955 (75).

Startling Stories (British)
No 17, March 1954 (93).

Superlove (Danish)
No 25, Oct 1969 (119).

Thrilling Wonder Stories
Winter 1954 (95); Summer 1954 (126).

Unearth
Winter 1979, Vol 2 No 4 (105).

Univers (French)
No 11, 1952 (?) (9); No 12, 1953 (?) (94); No 10, 1955 (?) (140).

Urania (Italian)
No 59, 1954 (22); No 72, 1955 (17); No 336, 1964 (142); No 359, 1964 (109); No 372, 1965 (92); No 385, 1965 (71); No 452, 1967 (48); No 466, 1967 (18); No 473, 1967 (64); No 490, 1968 (143); No 520, 1969 (141); No 534, 1969 (?) (29).

Vector (British)
No 64, March-April 1973 (6).

Vertex
Feb 1974 (57-a); Oct 1974 (85).

Victor B. Andersen's Maskinfabrik (Danish)
No 4, 1976 (134).

Voice
17 Jan 1974, Vol 55 No 14 (124).

Worlds Of Tomorrow
Aug 1963 (5); Oct 1963 (5); Dec 1963 (5); June 1964 (144); Aug 1964 (63); Jan 1965 (103); Nov 1965 (98); Jan 1966 (98); May 1966 (48).

The Yuba City High Times
20 Feb 1981 (4).

WORKS ABOUT PHILIP K DICK

This section is incomplete, but then there is no intention that it be otherwise. It is merely intended to list some representative works about Philip K Dick for the interested reader.

1. "Even Sheep Can Upset Scientific Detachment", Philip Purser, The Daily Telegraph Magazine, No 506, 19 July 1974.*

2. "The Ideos [sic] Cosmos Of Philip K Dick", Charles Platt, Ad Astra, Vol 1 No 6, 1979.*

3. "Into the Electronic Future", THE CYBERNETIC IMAGINATION IN SCIENCE FICTION, Patricia S Warrick, The MIT Press, Cambridge ($15.00), 1980.*

4. "The Labyrinthian Process Of The Artificial: Dick's Androids And Mechanical Constructs", Patricia S Warrick, Extrapolation, Summer 1979, Vol 20 No 2.*

5. "Phil Dick: Cult Star In A Martian Sky", Thomas M Disch, Crawdaddy, Dec 1975.*

6. "Philip K. Dick: A Parallax View", Terrence M Green, Science Fiction Review, No 17, May 1976.*

7. PHILIP K DICK: ELECTRIC SHEPHERD, Ed by Bruce Gillespie, Norstrilia Press, 1975, paper.*
   Contains: "Philip K Dick: Electric Shepherd", Roger Zelazny; "Foreword", Bruce Gillespie; "Mad, Mad Worlds: Seven Novels Of Philip K Dick", Bruce Gillespie; "Contradictions", Bruce Gillespie; "The Real Thing", Bruce Gillespie; "Now Wait For Last Year", George Turner; "Philip K Dick Saying It All Over Again", George Turner; "The Android And The Human", Philip K Dick; "Science Fiction: A Hopeless Case—With Exceptions", Stanislaw Lem; "Philip K Dick By 1975: Flow My Tears, The Policeman Said", George Turner; two Letters Of Comment by Philip K Dick and one by George Turner.

8. PHILIP K DICK—MATERIALIEN, Science Fiction Times, Special Issue No 1, 1976, paper.*
   Written in German.

9. PHILIP K. DICK & THE UMBRELLA OF LIGHT, Angus Taylor, T-K Graphics: SF Author Studies 1, 1975, paper.*

10. "The Politics Of Space, Time And Entropy", Angus Taylor, Foundation No 10, June 1976.*

11. "Science Fiction As Prophesy [sic]: Philip K. Dick", Ursula K Le Guin, New Republic, 30 Oct 1976.*

12. Science-Fiction Studies, No 5, Vol 2 Part 1, March 1975.*
    Special Philip K Dick issue.
    Contains: "P.K. Dick's Opus: Artifice As Refuge And World View", Darko Suvin; "Dick And Meta-SF", Carlo Pagetti; "After Armageddon: Character Systems In Dr. Bloodmoney", Frederic Jameson;

"Dick's Maledictory Web: About And Around Martian Time Slip", Brian W Aldiss; "Ubik: The Deconstruction Of Bourgeois SF", Peter Fitting; "Philip K. Dick: A Visionary Among The Charlatans", Stanislaw Lem; "Le Guin's Lathe Of Heaven And The Role Of Dick: The False Reality As Mediator", Ian Watson.

13. THE SPLINTERED SHARDS: REALITY AND ILLUSTION IN THE NOVELS OF PHILIP K. DICK, Claudia Krenz Bush, Master's Thesis (112 pages), Idaho State University, 1975.*

14. "The Sunstruck Forest", Anthony Wolk, Foundation, No 18, Jan 1980.

15. "The Swiss Connection: Psychological Systems In Philip K. Dick", Anthony Wolk, Mosaic, 1980.

16. "The Worlds Of Philip K Dick", John Brunner, New Worlds, No 166, Sept 1966.

17. "The Worlds Of Philip K. Dick", Paul Williams, Rolling Stone, 6 Nov 1975.*

See also numbers 52, 57, 62, 66, 70, 85, 107, 112, 135, and 148 in the STORIES section of this bibliography. And particularly, the introductions in the Gregg Press editions of numbers 4, 7, 13, 15, 18, 21, 23, 38, 40, 41, 42, 46, 48, and 49 in the BOOKS section of this bibliography.

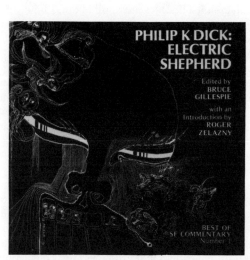

item 7.

item 9.

AFTERWORD

by Philip K Dick

What I write about, I think, is belief, faith, trust . . . and the lack of all three. "A universe of cynicism and chaos," I once said about my first novel, SOLAR LOTTERY. For me, in each successive novel, the doubt—or rather lack of trust or faith—grows deeper. The split widens, that yawning gap in the earth, into which everything that matters can fall. And, in the novel, but less openly, I explore the possibilities for a rebirth of faith. The yawning gap is the question; new faith is the answer. But faith in what?

The Universe disintegrates further and further in each of my novels, but the possibility of faith in one given human being or several—this faith is about certain distinct human beings: Molinari in NOW WAIT FOR LAST YEAR, Runciter in UBIK, Leo Bulero in THE THREE STIGMATA, and so forth. The redeemer exists; he lives; he can be found—usually—in the novel somewhere, at the centre of the stage or at the very edge. In some of the novels he merely lurks. He is implicit. But I believe in him completely. He is the friend who ultimately comes . . . and in time.

Basically, he is found at the heart of human life itself. He is, in fact, the heart of human life. He is the most alive of all. Where the chattering, bickering, sweating, planning, worrying, scheming centre of life holds sway—well, I have faith that he is there and will show himself, countering the process of entropy, of decay, that more and more undermines the universe itself. Stars are snuffed out; planets die into darkness and cold; but there in the marketplace of some small moon, he is busy formulating a plan for action—action against the black counterforce, the Palmer Eldritch figure in all his horrid manifestations.

In THE MAN IN THE HIGH CASTLE he is Mr Tagomi, a minor Japanese official in Japanese-occupied San Francisco. Mr Tagomi, in a moment of irritation and awareness of suffocation, refuses to sign a form which will transfer a certain Jew from Japanese authority to German authority—one life is saved, a small life and saved by a small life. But the enormous process of decline is pushed back slightly. Enough so that it matters. What Mr Tagomi has done matters. In a sense, there is nothing more important on all Earth than Mr Tagomi's irritable action.

I know only one thing about my novels. In them, again and again, this minor man asserts himself in all his hasty, sweaty strength. In the ruins of Earth's cities he is busily constructing a little factory that turns out cigars or maps or imitation artifacts that say, "Welcome to Miami, the pleasure center of the world." In "A Lincoln, Simulacrum", he operates a little business that produces corny electronic organs—and, later on, human-like robots which ultimately become more of an irritation than a threat. Everything is on a small scale. Collapse is enormous; the positive little figure outlined against the universal rubble is, like Tagomi, Runciter, Molinari, gnat-sized in scope, finite in what he can do . . . and yet in some sense great. I really do not know why. I simply believe in him, and I love him. He will prevail. There is nothing else. At least nothing else that matters. That we should be concerned about. Because if he is there, like a tiny father-figure, everything is all right.

Some reviewers have found "bitterness" in my writing. I am surprised, because my mood is one of trust. Perhaps they are bothered by the fact that what I trust is so very small. They want something vaster. I have news for them: there is nothing vaster. Nothing *more*, I should say. But, really, how much do we have to have. Isn't Mr Tagomi enough? Isn't what he does enough? I know it counts. I am satisfied.

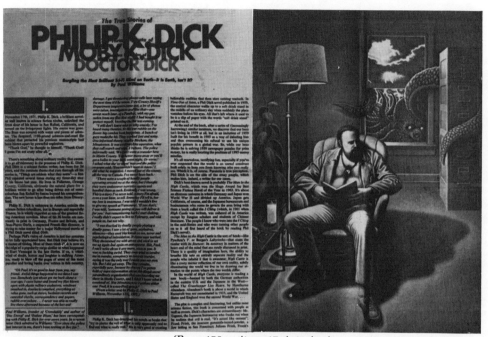

(Page 153 — item 17, interior.)

ACKNOWLEDGEMENTS

The compiler wishes to thank the following persons and organizations who supplied help and information for this bibliography.

> Debbie Notkin, Tom Whitmore, Charles N Brown, Paul Williams, Mark Hurst, Larry Paschelke and Jean-Pierre Moumon, for general help.
> Steve Godersky, who annotated the citations and whose collection is reproduced here in photographs.
> Paul Nelson for taking the many pictures used.
> Leone Umbaldi for extensive Italian coverage.
> Kurt Cockrum, who had a major influence on form and content.
> Bruce E Pelz and the Institute for Specialized Literature, Inc for help with fanzine publication data.

Jeff Levin, for typesetting the book, proof reading it, physically confirming a number of items, finding some additional printings, and resolving some confusing points.

Linda Herman and the California State University, Fullerton, Library, Special Collections Section for allowing access to the Philip K Dick collection and for making some suggestions of format which were incorporated.

Russell Galen, Jonathan Silverman and the Scott Meredith Literary Agency for providing data and help on foreign editions when Phil Dick asked them to help in this area.

Tim Underwood for designing the book and bringing it to fruition, and, most importantly, for initiating the entire project.

My wife, Sandra, for putting up with this, my second aberration, particularly when knowing that it does not end here.

And, finally, Philip K Dick for allowing examinations of his own books, magazines, and fanzines; for giving of his time to answer the many questions which came up in the course of preparing this bibliography; for his candidness in supplying pseudonymns and information about odd publication events; for the use of some of his works, for the Afterword and story notes—and simply for 30 years of writing.

PKD: A Philip K. Dick Bibliography
by Daniel J H Levack

This first edition is published in October, 1981, limited to 800 softbound and 300 hardcover copies. The hardcover copies were signed by author Philip K Dick, compiler Daniel J H Levack and annotator Steven Owen Godersky. Photography by Paul A Nelson. Halftone reproductions by Circus Lithograph, with technical assistance by Bud Birkenseer. Text paper is 60# Warrens "1854", an acid-free stock with extended shelf life; typeface is Mallard II (a design based on Hermann Zapf's Melior) set on a Compugraphic EditWriter by Jeff Levin of Pendragon Graphics, Beaverton, Oregon. This book was printed, smyth-sewn and bound by Braun-Brumfield, Inc., Ann Arbor, Michigan, in connection with Paul de Fremery & Co., San Francisco, California.

Softcover: ISBN 0-934438-33-1 . . . . $ 7.95
Clothbound: ISBN 0-934438-34-X

We are in the process of publishing a matched series of illustrated science
fiction bibliographies, including, among others, the works of Jack Vance,
Roger Zelazny, Frank Herbert, Poul Anderson and L. Sprague de Camp. For
more information write:

UNDERWOOD/MILLER
239 N. 4th Street
Columbia, PA 17512

FUTURE
SCIENCE FICTION

NO. 29

35¢

VULCAN'S HAMMER

by PHILIP K. DICK

L. SPRAGUE de CAMP   RICHARD WILSON

RANDALL GARRETT   WALLACE WEST   and others

"Vulcan's Hammer" — first magazine appearance. (See page 131, item 138.a.)